Hovercraft
The Story of a Very British Invention

Arthur W. J. G. Ord-Hume

Hovercraft quickly developed into sophisticated pieces of equipment made to tackle specific tasks. Besides ferryboats across tricky terrain, they could be a positive boon to military operations. One maker, Vosper Thorneycroft, entered the Hovercraft market with a 'sidewall' machine. This was a variety of Hovercraft where the cushion of air supporting the vessel was retained by two rigid sides which, in water, stayed submerged. It was also driven by conventional propellers. This meant you could not drive it up a beach or across dry land. The company then made this one, the VT-2, which, unlike the earlier VT-1, was a proper free-floating Hovercraft. Highly manoeuvrable over shallow water, it was powered by a pair of 4,500 hp Rolls-Royce Marine Proteus gas turbines. See p.28.

Stenlake Publishing Ltd

© 2016 Arthur W. J. G. Ord-Hume
First Published in the United Kingdom, 2016
Stenlake Publishing Limited
54-58 Mill Square, Catrine, KA5 6RD
www.stenlake.co.uk

ISBN 9781840337389

Printed by
P2D Books,
1 Newlands Rd,
Westoning,
Bedford,
MK45 5LD

Bibliography

Cagle, Malcolm W: *Flying Ships: Hovercraft and Hydrofoils*. Dodd, Mead, New York, 1970

Cross, Ian, & O'Flaherty, C A: *Introduction to Hovercraft and Hoverports*. Pitman Publishing/Juanita Kalerghi, London, 1975

Elsley, G H, & Devereux, A J: *Hovercraft Design & Construction*. David & Charles, Newton Abbot, 1968

George, J M: *Future Hovercraft*. [lecture before Institute of Marketing entitled 'Tomorrow's Travel World ', London, October 31st, 1977

Gunston, [William Tudor] 'Bill': *Hydrofoils and Hovercraft*. Aldus Books, London, 1969

Hogg, Garry: *The Hover-Craft Story*. Abelard-Schuman, London, 1970

Hollebone, Ashley: *The Hovercraft Story*. The History Press, Stroud, Gloucestershire, 2011

Hollebone, Ashley: *The Hovercraft: A History*. The History Press, Stroud, Gloucestershire, 2012

Larsen, Egon: *Hovercraft & Hydrofoils Work like This*. Dent & Sons, London. 1970

Mackett, John: *The Portsmouth-Ryde Passage: A Personal View*. Ravensbourne Press, London, 1970

McLeavy, Roy: *Jane's Surface Skimmers: Hovercraft and Hydrofoils*. Eds. 1st&c (1970 - 1985). London, var.eds.

Ord-Hume, Arthur W J G: 'The Future of Hovercraft' (article), *Hoveringcraft & Hydrofoil*, July 1962, pp. 12-13

Paine, Robin, & Syms, Roger: *On a Cushion of Air: the Story of Hoverlloyd*. Writersworld, Oxfordshire, 2012

Watts, Anthony J: *A Source Book of Hydrofoils and Hovercraft*. Ward Lock Ltd, London, 1978

Wheeler, Raymond L, & Chaplin, J B: *In the Beginning: The SR-N1 Hovercraft*. Cross Print, Isle of Wight, 2007

Most definitely not a Hovercraft, this is a hydrofin travelling at speed riding on its fully-submerged hydrofin wings. Built in Hamburg by the Blohm+Voss company, the Dolphin-class vessel was built under licence from the Grumman Aircraft Engineering Corporation, It is powered by one 3,600 hp Rolls-Royce Tyne and a pair of General Motors diesels and 2 waterjets. The 83-ton vessel is 23m in length and can travel at 48 knots out of water or 8-10 knots when in the water. Built as a ferry to travel between the Spanish mainland and the Island of Majorca, the Las Palmas-based *Corsario Negro* is pictured here on pre-delivery trials in the Baltic in 1966. Capable of carrying 88 passengers in one cabin with a small kitchenette, it entered service with Maritima Antares on July 6th 1967, but the following year was sold to a South Florida ferry operator. Unlike a Hovercraft, the hydrofoil vessel was highly susceptible to water-state and became unreliable as a scheduled service operator. In 1970 it went to the US Navy.

Introduction

Sir Christopher Sydney Cockerell (1910-1999), the Cambridge-born inventor behind the Hovercraft. Educated at Gresham's and Peterhouse, Cambridge, Cockerell worked on radio research among other things and developed navigational equipment for Marconi. With a legacy left by his father he bought a small Norfolk boat and caravan hire business and launched upon a programme of boat-hull lubrication using air. The famous story of the 'first hovercraft' made from a vacuum cleaner and two empty food cans dates from 1955. He ceased hull experiments and concentrated on the Hovercraft. Like all British inventors from Frank Whittle upwards, Cockerell faced an uphill task in seeking backing for development work which he finally negotiated through the National Research Development Council in 1959 with a placing of a development contract with Saunders-Roe at Cowes. Cockerell was knighted in 1969.

The Hovercraft was a revolutionary invention that enjoyed an almost meteoric popularity. Then, almost as rapidly as it appeared on the scene, it waned and then, in the space of less than a half-century, it dwindled. Now it is almost forgotten.

Today it is seen as a specialised military vehicle and as a great sporting toy for the man who has everything else. In short, it's viewed as of limited importance. The three services have all evaluated the Hovercraft yet significantly there's now no great rush to introduce them.

For fast ferry-crossings of waterways and estuaries, transport across difficult and unprepared mixed terrain, there is no equal. The problem is that today there's a variety of means of attaining that end result – and the Hovercraft is only one of them.

But the sporting Hovercraft still exists up and down the country as do groups of enthusiasts who build and fly these practical miniature runabouts. Like the Autogiro, in some ways the designer's original idea remains unspoiled: it's only the more serious side to the whole thing that has been stripped back and chucked away leaving us with the 'fun' part of what once was being put forward as the next great transport revolution.

Make no mistake about it, though, the Hovercraft remains a unique vehicle in that nothing like it existed until its moment of invention – and then it caught on like wildfire as everybody thought up amazing uses for it in transport, commerce, combat, defence, rescue, sport and competition.

Unlike the motor car and the aeroplane before, it went from literally nothing to a state of total global acceptance virtually in the blink of an eye. It seemed that it was the answer to all our future transport needs.

Few could imagine that in less than half a century, Hovercraft would largely be forgotten and, after the lines of the Victorian charabanc, be considered an example of an out-dated technology that had passed its peak.

And because it was a British invention, its inventor was largely ignored in his lifetime and he died in, if not exactly poverty, then certainly with less money than would make a useful working wage.

But we are too far ahead of the story – there's the tale of a whole 50 years of development, expansion, exploitation and ultimate decline to relate.

In the summer of 1959 word got out that Saunders-Roe was building something unusual at its works on the River Medina at Cowes on the Isle of Wight. It was rumoured to be a new type of flying machine using an entirely new principle. Nobody knew much more than that. Light aircraft from Sandown Airport and Southampton's Eastleigh Aerodrome began taking a close interest in the huge hangars at East Cowes. Tipped off that the vast doors were opening and something was being pushed out, there was a rush to catch the first photograph… This turned out to be it. Fuzzy, short on detail and taken from a height of several thousand feet, this was the first sight the outside world had of the SR.N1 or 'Saunders-Roe Nautical-1'. Almost circular in planform it carried a 'landing pad' at each corner – one is just visible on the front of the Hovercraft at the lower

centre of this picture. It was the first Sunday in June. Later that day the SR.N1 started up its Alvis Leonides engine and three times rose 12 inches above the ground, notching up a total of half an hour of hovering flight. The press referred to it as 'Britain's Flying Saucer. ' Gosh! We were still a proud nation then.

What is a Hovercraft?

First of all, a basic fact about the name 'Hovercraft'. While the word 'Hovercraft' is now accepted as a generic name for any machine of this type, it should be remembered that 'Hovercraft' was originally a trade name (trademark) registered to and owned by Saunders-Roe Ltd, later known as British Hovercraft Corporation (BHC) Ltd, then Westland. This explains why other manufacturers strove to devise similar but alternative names for their air-cushion vehicles.

The Hovercraft is an amazingly simple device. So simple in fact that it seems curious it took so long before somebody 'invented' it.

In very simple but nevertheless accurate terms, cushion of air beneath an object creates lift which is then easily converted into directional motion either by a separate thruster (a propeller or a jet of air) or by directing part of the lifting air cushion to bleed away at an angle from beneath the craft. This is known as the ground-effect phenomenon. The cushion of air needs only to be of quite low pressure to do its job.

If this cushion is formed in a space comprising the whole underside of the craft, then this is called a plenum chamber, an expression taken from the Latin *plānus* meaning 'level' or 'flat'. There are variations. If the air pressure is directed through an annular duct beneath the craft this is often called the peripheral jet curtain suspension system. The third main category is where the bottom of the craft is closed off to a certain extent by a large number of open ended flexible tubes into which air is pumped. This is the pressure skirt system.

Whichever principle is applied, the effect is to raise the craft from the ground. Because the cushion of air is between the craft underside and the terrain beneath, this can be water, grass, mud, concrete, gravel or anything else. It is this ability to rise above the underlying surface that gives the Hovercraft its unique performance characteristics.

When first the Hovercraft appeared, those responsible for legislation had a field day! It flew in the air, so therefore the driver ought to be a licensed pilot. But it also operated on and over water, so therefore it was a boat and had to be operated by a licensed mariner.

Meanwhile the Royal Air Force said it wasn't an aircraft but a boat, and the Royal Navy said it wasn't a boat so therefore it must be an aeroplane. The Army reckoned it was a sort of Jeep so all you needed was a driving licence…

While the civil servants tasked with the job of pigeon-holing this strange new device argued endlessly as to what it might best be called, the rest of us accepted that the Hovercraft was a curious beast that existed somewhere between a four-wheel-drive car, a boat, an aircraft and a caterpillar-tracked vehicle for it could, seemingly, go everywhere and anywhere regardless of terrain.

Enthusiasts are often blind to the obvious and, like the myrmidons of Whitehall ministries, we tend to see only what we would like to see.

The Hovercraft operates in air close to the ground which renders the vessel more dependent on the science of aeronautics than hydronamics. The Hovercraft's big advantage is that, like the four-wheel drive all-terrain vehicle, it can traverse all types of terrain, rough, smooth, wet, dry, powdery, rocky or overgrown. It is not susceptible to excursions in the terrain meaning that it can pass over sharp depressions and protrusions, ruts and rocks smoothly without imparting spine-jolting loads to the spines on its passengers. While boats, including punts and flat-bottomed vessels, need some water in which to operate in shallows, the Hovercraft operates above the surface and can be described as a 'zero-draft' vessel.

What a Hovercraft isn't

There are definitely a few things that the Hovercraft is not and it is as well to consider these here as well. They range from Hydrofins through to the famed Caspian Sea Monsters of the Soviet Cold War.

There is a tendency for non-technicians to lump together the three popular types of over-water craft and call them 'Hovercraft' whereas the pure Hovercraft may only be considered in isolation. Air cushion vehicles are divided into two principal categories – side-wall craft and full Hovercraft. The latter is fully flexible and will traverse all types of terrain and water in all directions, while the side-wall craft is only suitable for use on water because of its rigid sides to the hull. The cushion of air is formed and deployed between rigid sides which are submerged at all times.

Still lacking any dedicated means of forward propulsion, the SR.N1 as seen from the ground. The chequerboard rudders, four positioned in fore-and-aft pairs, are seen together with the two very tall vertical fins for direction stabilisation. These rudders and fins were too close-coupled to be of much good as would soon become obvious. Notice that both ends are quite rounded.

The third category is the Hydrofoil which, as we have already seen, is not an air-cushion vehicle.

Yet another type of craft is the ground-effect vehicle and here the definition lies in the title. Within the heading of G-EVs we find such specialist transport vessels as the Russian Ekranoplans and their like.

Let's start with Hydrofins and Hydrofoils. While it may also depend to a greater or lesser extent on the build-up of air pressure under the hull, the hydrofin is nothing like the Hovercraft in its means of operation. Here we have what resembles a conventional boat hull but beneath it is a structure of specially-shaped slats which are *foils* – shaped lifting surfaces. As these pass through the water, they exert a lifting force on the array of foils which, as the hull accelerates, reduces the drag and lifts the hull out of the water.

In its developed form, the hydrofin comprises an array of special 'wings' or 'foils' (think of them as 'aerofoils' that work in water) beneath the hull of the craft so arranged that the faster the vessel fitted with them travels, the more 'lift' is provided by these hydrofoil wings until the whole hull may be carried out of the water, the hull sitting on the very small low-drag profile of a hydrofoil.

The man who pioneered the practical hydrofin was Christopher Hook. His final craft, the HN-4, was powered by a Pobjoy radial aircraft engine driving a four-bladed propeller from a Monospar aircraft. Extending in front of the hull on two curved arms was a pair of airfoil-shaped predictors and another beneath the tail. These 'read' the sea-state and automatically adjusted the incidence of the main hydrofoil so that it remained virtually a constant depth beneath the surface.

The Hook Hydrofin was built on the Isle of Wight by Ron Benton (later of Britten-Norman) in the summer of 1948 and was tried out in the Solent waters off Wootton Creek before being taken to America for extended further trials.

What would go down in history as the world's first Hovercraft was the Saunders-Roe SR.N1 built at Cowes on the Isle of Wight. Here it is being demonstrated under its 'B' Conditions markings G-12-4 in lieu of an aircraft civil registration. This skirtless Hovercraft is seen hovering at the 1959 Farnborough air show with a full complement of 20 marines on board. Note the added nose structure to extend the original circular planform of the vessel.

Hydrofins are in general classified as 'surface skimmers' and 'fly' their hulls clear of the water surface when at speed. But they are not Hovercraft. Furthermore, the small airfoils upon which they 'fly' in the water are prone to damage from floating detritus. You can lift a hydrofoil craft straight out of the water with a crane – but you may not beach one!

The hydrofin makes for a fast and stable ferry-boat or other form of sea transport but relies on forward speed for its performance as distinct from static lift.

Ground-effect vehicles (G-EVs) are a curious byway of the lifting-surface principle. Although they include impressive-looking vessels such as the gigantic Ekranoplans for the former Soviet Union, they are, however, not to be confused with the real Hovercraft. An Ekranoplan generates its lift aerodynamically by travelling at speed though the air very close to the ground. It cannot hover or stop in the air but must accelerate to the point where its body and form can create aerodynamic lift beneath it. The Ekranoplan flies in the air, albeit at very low altitude and only in that narrow band of air known as ground effect or ground cushion.

A Quick History of Ground-Effect Vehicles.

For a very long time it has been known that the speed and efficiency of a boat can be improved by lubricating its passage through water with a thin film of air. Expressed another way, the drag of a surface through water can be lowered by blowing air onto its surface.

This use of air as a lubricant had been known for some while, although the thought of using it is a supporting cushion for a vessel was untried. The engineer and boat-builder Sir John Isaac Thorneycroft (1845-1928) had experimented with air-lubricated boat hulls in the mid-1870s with the sole effort of reducing drag and increasing hull efficiency but he was hampered by available materials and process technology.

A Russian engineer named Vladimir Israilevich Levkov experimented during the mid-1930s with what was very nearly the first Hovercraft vehicle but having gone so far with his research, the project seems officially to have been rejected and further development ceased. This was despite having apparently successfully designed a high-speed motor torpedo-boat. It did not, however, make use of an air cushion.

More work on ships followed, in particular by a Finnish engineer, Toivo Jujani Kaario (1912-1970) who, in 1931, designed an air-cushion vehicle which he built and allegedly tested. He was granted a patent for this but had no funding for further development and it seems that the advantage that he may have had was allowed to escape.

In more recent times, there has been a more serious challenge to the kudos of Hovercraft invention and this heralded from the United Sates. During the Second World War, a United States Navy reservist named Charles J Fletcher designed a vehicle which he named a 'Glidemobile'. The device appears to have worked by the entrapment of a constant volume of air between the underside of the Glidemobile and the upper side of the surface beneath, this volume of air being provided from a compressor or static source and acting against a uniform surface, either the ground or water, providing anywhere from ten inches to two feet of lift to free it from the surface. Control of the craft was achieved by the measured release of air in a predetermined direction.

What happened next is almost a carbon-copy of the way Cockerell's invention was treated in Britain. Shortly after being tested on Beezer's Pond in Fletcher's home town of Sparta Township, New Jersey, the design was immediately appropriated by the United States Department of War and classified as 'secret', denying Fletcher the opportunity to patent his creation.

This virtually ensured that Fletcher's work remained largely unknown until a case was brought (British Hovercraft Ltd v. The United States of America) in which the British corporation maintained that its rights, coming from Sir Christopher Cockerell's patent, had been infringed. British Hovercraft's claim, seeking $104,000,000 in damages, was unsuccessful. However, one Colonel Melville Whitnel Beardsley (1913-1998), an American inventor and aeronautical engineer, received $80,000 from Cockerell for his rights to American patents.

It now seems certain that both Beardsley and Cockerell conceived the idea of the air-cushion vehicle independently and at virtually the same time. Had the US Government not suppressed this knowledge it might well have been a totally different story.

Beardsley is understood to have worked on a number of unique ideas in the 1950s and '60s which he patented. He is later thought to have worked for the US Navy on the development of Hovercraft for military use.

In 1952 the British inventor Christopher Cockerell worked with air lubrication with test craft on the Norfolk Broads. From this he moved on to the idea of a definable air cushion. Cockerell experimented with a vacuum cleaner motor and two cylindrical cans to create his unique peripheral jet system, the key to his Hovercraft invention. He established the workable principle of a vehicle suspended on a cushion of air blown out under pressure, making the vehicle easily mobile over most surfaces. The supporting air cushion would enable it to operate over soft mud, water, and marshes and swamps as well as on firm ground. He designed a working model vehicle based on his patent. Showing his model to the authorities proved an ill-advised move for they immediately put it on the 'secret' list as being of possible military use and therefore restricted.

In 1955 Cockerell succeeded in convincing the Ministry of Supply to back him but he was hamstrung in his attempts to move the project forward commercially thanks its having been placed on the government's restricted classification because of its potential military benefits.

It was four long years before Cockerell managed to get his idea removed from the secret list, whereupon he immediately formed the Hovercraft Development Company Ltd.

Possibly aware that there were others around the world with similar ideas, and in an effort to keep Britain in the lead in developments, funding equal to £150,000 was available from the National Research and Development Corporation to take on his design and a contract to build an experimental prototype was awarded to Saunders Roe, the old-established flying-boat firm at Cowes. This would become the SR.N1.

The vessel was built to Cockerell's design and was launched in 1959, undertaking a crossing of the English Channel from France to the UK on the 50th anniversary of Blériot's cross-Channel flight.

The SR.N1 in its original form takes to the open sea in moderate conditions – but still had difficulty proceeding in a straight line. Once proceeding in a predetermined direction it would more or less keep going but more often that not it would gently drift to one side and require rather more than normal skills to coax it back onto course.

Conquering the Playpen Effect: the Skirt is Born!

Hovercraft altitude remains a function of the amount of air being pumped under the craft by compressor fans. And because it was free to escape all the way around the craft's underside, that altitude was rather restricted. Twelve inches was very good, six to nine inches average. Rough terrain meant an awful lot of hard bumping into protrusions.

The engineer saw all the advantages of the Hovercraft – but could also identify some pretty serious disadvantages. Now while there was nothing really wrong with a flying-machine where you measured altitude with a dip-stick, the Hovercraft relied on that slender cushion of air beneath it and this was easily compromised by irregularities in the surface over which it was being operated. A rough sea ensured a rough ride as the waves challenged the air cushion, and a few large stones on the ground scraped the bottom of the hull regardless of the cushion.

Christopher Cockerell understood these limitations and experimented with the obvious solution – a greater cushion of air to raise the vessel higher. This worked quite well but if the vessel was moving forwards at speed, it was possible to 'fall off the cushion' and tip the Hovercraft's nose into the water or ground. While not itself a serious problem, it could be very uncomfortable for anybody on the Hovercraft when it tipped forward and virtually stopped.

An article by the present author was published in the magazine *Hovering Craft & Hydrofoil* in which these problems were discussed. This characteristic was referred to as 'the playpen problem' for the Hovercraft's territory, theoretically boundless, was anything but and could be contained by the slenderest of barriers.

In an amusing and revealing correspondence between Cockerell and the author, the former conceded that this playpen effect was both real and challenging. We projected a variety of solutions. A simple answer would have been to increase the power into the compressing fan but this would have been highly expensive

Bearing the markings of the National Research Development Council the diminutive SR.N1 was demonstrated on the River Thames to Members of Parliament and Commonwealth Prime Ministers on May 24th, 1960. The main lift engine was an Alvis Leonides radial. *Picture by Ronald A Cole.*

On July 25th, 1959, the SR.N1 crossed the English Channel from Calais to Dover for the first time. Transported there as deck cargo on a ship, the craft departed Calais at 4.49 a.m. and arrived at Dover at 6.45. It had been a rough crossing with a number of interruptions, but it was a successful 'first'. Here, parked at a racy angle on Dover's shingle, the Hovercraft rests after its historic trip. The crew was Peter 'Sheepy' Lamb, pilot, John Chaplin (head of research) and, as passenger, Christopher Cockerell. It was the 50th anniversary of Blériot's crossing of the Channel, also from France to England.

---

as regards fuel consumed and since you would probably not need maximum power at all times (such as when traversing somewhere smooth), the control system would become over-complex with sensors and predictors 'reading' the terrain ahead. More power was a simple answer but, on so many counts, no more than a 'last-ditch' action.

It was Cockerell himself who came up with a potentially practical solution in the form of what he called 'a web' but, perhaps surprisingly, this proved to be rather a way down his list of priorities.

A whole raft of engineers, entranced by the potential of the Hovercraft, were now addressing this problem, besides the present author who, as managing director and chief designer to Phoenix Aircraft Ltd, built and experimented with a small Hovercraft equipped with an all-round skirt cut from sheet rubber. Immediately, the model was lifted well clear of the surface but the transition to lateral movement meant that the skirt was subjected to loads which could (and did) rupture it. The first trial took place on March 29th, 1960, at 15.45 hrs.

Quite rapidly, my 'web' became 'the skirt' and it progressed from being a single band of semi-tensioned rubber sheet to an overlapping array of interlocking rubber pockets or fingers which could be inflated by the air pressure of the plenum chamber and, as they were open at the bottom, could direct a stabilising curtain of air inwards to help contain the plenum chamber while at the same time forming a flexible peripheral 'comb' which contained the cushion of air and allowed the Hovercraft to clear obstructions up to half the height of the hull. As obstructions were encountered, the semi-rigid inflated segments were deflected out of the way without venting a large area of the air cushion though a large gap.

One of my co-directors, Cecil Hugh Latimer-Needham (1900-1975), had been a highly-talented aircraft designer in pre-war days. The holder of the first glider pilot's licence in Britain, he pioneered the revival of the gliding movement in 1930 and during the war played an important part in the development of air-crew life-rafts, a skill which gave him unparalleled experience of working with rubberised cloth. He was also a pioneer in the field of in-flight refuelling.

Latimer-Needham witnessed some of my Hovercraft skirt trials in my blister hangar at Panshanger Aerodrome in Hertfordshire as a result of which he took it upon himself to apply for the first British patent to cover a Hovercraft skirt. He did this in his own name and not in that of the company.

Crucially, and as now is clear to see, he only understood the outline of the skirt theory, not the detail and application. As a consequence, his patent was both incomplete and as with other patents that attempt to embrace too wide a spectrum, too general to be useful – even to Saunders-Roe who bought it.

Of course, because it was a 'maiden patent' on a subject, it would have required an expensive additional patent to include the steerable or focusing skirt which I demonstrated later to both Christopher Cockerell and Saunders-Roe.

This action was unfortunate in that Latimer-Needham had not fully understood the technology behind my 'overlapping fingers' and so the patent he was awarded completely missed out on the key element of the practical skirt. It was, though, the very first skirt patent and he subsequently managed to sell it and the rights to its use to Saunders-Roe. By the time that had happened, however, engineers from Cowes had visited Panshanger and seen my model demonstrated.

The introduction of structures to the front and rear of the SR.N1 served two purposes. First they were an attempt to improve the directional stability of the craft and, second, to trial the hull planform for the SR.N2. In this photograph can be seen the jet engine placed at the rear to provide additional forward thrust.

Invention and Inventors

Having established the probability that the Hovercraft was thought up in two places at once, there arises the possibility that there was even more to it than that.

It is a sad fact of life that whoever invents anything, somebody else will attempt to bend history to prove that they invented it earlier than the published claim! For a long while this was the prerogative of our Soviet friends who, so they claimed, pioneered just about everything before anybody else. Now it has spread to other countries including our transatlantic cousins in America.

An Illinois physician named William Bertelsen published a claim in a US magazine in the mid-1960s that he had built a Hovercraft-type flying car. As the years went by, though, the 'mid-1960s' tended to become 'mid-1950s' as Dr. Bertelsen laid claim to having built the first man-carrying Hovercraft.

In fact, Bertelsen's Hovercraft – he named it the Aeromobile – was built in 1959 and demonstrated before the American press on October 23rd of that year. This was four full years after Christopher Cockerell had successfully built and operated his first model. Cockerell would be knighted in 1969 for his services to engineering.

It is considered nevertheless that Dr Bertelsen was indeed the first American to build and fly a man-carrying Hovercraft. Born in 1920, Bertelsen continued perfecting his Aeromobile Model 35B up to the time of his death in 2009. He received no US government funding for his efforts. Nor did he use a flexible skirt.

So what about the inventor of the Hovercraft as we know him? Here I can do little better than quote from the very fulsome tribute written by Michael T Kaufman upon the death of Sir Christopher Cockerell aged 88 years in 1999:

With the Marboré jet engine at the rear, the SR.N1 conducted most of its early trials in the waters between Cowes and Nettlestone. Here east of Ryde Pier, the Hovercraft is making heavy weather of the shallows off Appley Beach. Note the frame protruding from the front end which carries a pitot head for the measurement of airspeed. The correct calibration of Hovercraft speed was an early challenge for Saunders-Roe which discovered, not unexpectedly, that the pitching of the craft generated an inaccurate reading when using an airspeed indicator and that a water-speed indicator was more reliable.

At the conclusion of the first Channel crossing by Hovercraft on July 25th, 1959, the SR.N1 arrives at Dover. Not too many people were present to witness history in the making.

'Sir Christopher had hundreds of patents to his name, including more than 50 associated with the Hovercraft. Since the launching of his first Hovercraft, exactly 40 years before the day of his death, the technology that he made possible emerged from what seemed to be science fiction to become a common means of speedily ferrying passengers across bays and rivers around the world.

'Although Sir Christopher received great recognition and knighthood, he consistently vented his frustration at the lack of rewards he gained. He also criticized British policies that he contended chronically thwarted technological development and discouraged inventions and inventors.

'I've enjoyed life,' Sir Christopher said in an interview in 1996. 'But it would have been nice to treat my wife to dinner once in a while.' Actually, his patents did provide what he conceded was a reasonable living, but they did not make him rich.

'He moved to Norfolk to manage a marina on the Oulton Broad. A passionate sailor, he lived in a trailer and designed cabin cruisers. It was there that he conceived the idea that even a heavy craft could be supported on a cushion of air generated by relatively small thrust. Cutting the friction between boat and water, or boat and marshland, would allow such a vessel to move swiftly. He ran a vacuum cleaner tube through an empty can of cat food that he had placed in a larger empty coffee can and when he turned the switch to reverse to blow air into the larger can, the smaller one hovered.

'In 1955, he built a two-foot prototype that scooted at the end of a leash over water and land, and he obtained a patent for a vehicle that he described as 'neither an airplane, nor a boat, nor a wheeled land craft.' He named it a Hovercraft.

'There was little smooth sailing, however, as Sir Christopher sought to turn his idea into a commercial project. At one point he demonstrated his hovering prototype for British military officials who responded by classifying his invention as secret, effectively freezing development.

Hovercraft prototype G-12-4, better known as the SR.N4, underwent many changes in its career. Mostly these changes concerned manoeuvrability and attempts to make more precise directional control. One of these was to install a Viper jet engine for forward thrust. In this form it was known as the Mk.3 and it is seen here making the transition from the sea to the hard standing at Lee-on-Solent's HMS *Daedalus* naval base.

'Sir Christopher pawned family jewellery to keep his research going, and in 1957, after he had advised Government officials that the Swiss were working on hovering technologies, he was able to approach the National Research Development Corporation, a Government-financed agency that was supposed to promote inventions.

'Two years later, the agency formed Hovercraft Development Ltd to develop the concept for commercial use and solicit investment. Mr. Cockerell became a director and technical adviser.

'Hovercraft Development licensed five companies to build Hovercrafts. On June 1, 1959, a small one-person vehicle zipped across the English Channel in 20 minutes, four hours faster than conventional crossings. In the next three years, larger Hovercraft built by contractors began to carry passengers.

'In the mid-60s, as Hovercraft began commercial service across the Channel, Mr. Cockerell found himself in violent disagreement with management decisions by the Research Development Corporation. First he objected to a decision to license foreign companies, principally in the United States and Japan, allowing them to produce Hovercraft in exchange for royalties.

'That, he felt, only squandered Britain's advantage. He also opposed a directive in 1966 that fused all British Hovercraft development in one amalgamated company. Saying that move hampered competition and would 'stultify the hovercraft industry in Britain,' Sir Christopher resigned from Hovercraft Development in protest.

'Reflecting on the pitfalls of an inventor's life in Britain then, he wrote: 'Everything is stacked against you, but for some reason some silly chaps seem to be driven to it (rather like a painter or a composer of music), which is perhaps just as well or we should still be living in the Stone Age. Some of the Hovercraft saga was fun, but most of it was incredibly frustrating.'

In 1969 he was knighted, and the next year the British Hovercraft industry dismissed him as a consultant. He continued to lecture on the technology that he developed and conducted research at his home.

This resumé paints a dismal picture of the way we treat our inventors. Were it not for the fact that this is no isolated instance, we might savour complacency. This, though, is so often the story that the realms of coincidence no longer offer even the randomness of mere coincidence and we are left to face the stark truth that we wouldn't recognise a pioneer if he was neon-signed in our own front gardens!

But now it's time to chart the official path of the air-cushion vehicle.

Airline pilot or sea captain – the argument rumbles on!

As I showed earlier, the early Hovercraft confused those in High Places who realised that it existed somewhere between a four-wheel-drive car, a boat and an aircraft. Because it was vessel that could ply for hire and reward, you needed to be able to licence the 'driver'! The fundamental question, though, was what exactly was it the driver drove?

In fact, when first it appeared in the 1950s, so unsure were the authorities as to which regime it ought to occupy, that it was proclaimed that to drive one you had to be a licensed aircraft pilot and must hold a commercial pilot's licence before you carried passengers. Then it was pointed out that the vessel could work at sea so therefore you had to have nautical training and be a qualified ship's captain.

Fortunately for the sanity of all concerned, it was finally accepted that Hovercraft are vehicles closer to aircraft than ships but as they operate at height measured in inches, you could hardly call them aircraft. Sure, for carrying passengers and operating commercially, you must have a commercial operators' licence but for all else, and this includes the large sporting area of the Hovercraft market, you need merely common-sense. Insurance might be seen as a prudent extra…

The Hovercraft operates in air close to the ground which renders the vessel more dependent on the science of aeronautics than hydronamics. The Hovercraft's big advantage is that, like the four-wheel drive all-terrain vehicle, it can traverse all types of terrain, rough, smooth, wet, dry, powdery, rocky or overgrown. It is not susceptible to excursions in the terrain meaning that it can pass over sharp depressions and protrusions, ruts and rocks smoothly without imparting spine-jolting loads to the spines of its passengers. While boats, including punts and flat-bottomed vessels, need some water in which to operate in shallows, the Hovercraft operates above the surface and can be described as a 'zero-draft' vessel.

Again, this should not be confused with the popular zero-draft aero-engine and propeller-driven high-speed rafts used in swamp areas of America such as Florida's Everglades, or the ice and snow-traversing surface boats from above the Arctic Circle.

Military Trials and Applications

The military potential of the Hovercraft became evident after the first demonstrations of Hovercraft during 1959 and 1960. In February 1962 the Interservice Hovercraft Trials Unit (IHTU) was established at HMS *Daedalus* (at that time called HMS *Ariel*). Almost 13 years later, on December 31st, 1974, the Interservice Hovercraft Unit (IHU) was disbanded with the withdrawal of Army and Royal Air Force support. The role of the IHU was then taken over by the Naval Hovercraft Trials Unit formed on January 1st, 1975.

Between 1974 and 1976, the Unit was commanded by Bill Hart (1927-2014), a former Fleet Air Arm pilot, who once asserted, tongue firmly in cheek, that as the British had invented the tank, the steam engine, London taxis and wet weather, it was only natural that they should combine the qualities of all of these in the Hovercraft!

To begin with, IHTU's evaluation of Hovercraft was carried out on craft hired from their manufacturers but in 1964 it was decided to purchase the craft to be used for these trials. Trials have been conducted in no fewer than 22 countries in different climates and over a wide variety of terrains. Among the earliest of these overseas detachment was to the Far East and resulted in the formation of the Army's 200 Hovercraft Squadron. The original trials craft were the SR.N3 and the SR.N5 but subsequently SR.N6 and BH.7 were added to the fleet of craft based at Lee-on-Solent.

There's something about an American which makes them want the biggest and best that choice (or natural selection) will allow. And that's the way it was with passenger Hovercraft. It was February 25th, 1959, when somebody in Chicago, Illinois, saw details of Christopher Cockerell's invention and read an article which I had written for a US popular mechanics' magazine. Nobody was quite sure what a Hovercraft was and I had been invited to explain, in rudimentary terms, how one operated. I wrote of Hovercraft able to carry 100 passengers. Then this artists' impression appeared headed 'skimming saucer' suggesting a 40,000-ton vessel 330 feet in diameter accommodating 1,000 passengers riding eight feet above the sea on a cushion of air. There was, of course, no skirt. I have no doubt it gave somebody a vicarious thrill but it was all pie in the sky.

IHTU and its successor IHU was also responsible for the training of all military Hovercraft pilots and navigators while it was also a first-rate opportunity to train technical and stores personnel in servicing and stores maintenance.

Personnel were drawn from the Royal Navy, the Royal Marines, the Royal Air Force and the Army.

The military trials which took place in the 1970s showed how useful such a vehicle might be in the landing of troops on beach-heads and the positioning of equipment over terrain unsuited to any other form of vehicle.

The Hovercraft played a useful part in the Falklands War when two Royal Navy SR.N6 machines were used to patrol in inland waters during the conflict.

Passenger-carrying and Freight

It was as a cross-Channel vehicle and passenger-carrier that the Hovercraft came into its own. And, by a curious quirk of events, not only was this its finest hour but the start of its demise. It all began in 1965 with the setting up of British Rail Hovercraft Ltd. This created Seaspeed, a joint Hovercraft operation company formed by British Rail and the French railway operator, SNCF. Seaspeed was to operate a cross-Channel passenger and car service between Dover and Calais and Boulogne-sur-Mer using two SR.N4 Hovercraft. The passenger service started in 1966 and in August 1968 it took delivery of two new machines to carry cars as well as people. These were named *The Princess Margaret* and *The Princess Anne*.

Eight years later, both these craft were rebuilt to insert a 56 feet long plug to extend the hull length which increased passenger capacity from 254 to 418 while allowing the car capacity to rise to 60 vehicles. These two extended Hovercraft gave almost faultless service on this popular route, able to cross the Channel at up to 60 knots in little more than 30 minutes.

During its existence, in 1981 the original Seaspeed merged with its rival, Hoverlloyd, so creating Hoverspeed.

But the idea of a tunnel under the Channel – one was actually begun in Napoleonic times – became reality in 1994 and the competition for the cross-Channel service increased by a number of notches. The sad truth about cross-Channel operations lay in the fact that, contrary to what economists and accountants had been forecasting, and in spite of transporting 1.25m people and their motorcars, profit margins were small.

But there were still grand ideas for extending the principles of the Hovercraft. Christopher Cockerell, left, discusses his latest project, a Hovertrain, with project engineer Alan Pennington as they stand by a model of the train at Hovercraft Headquarters at Hythe, Kent, on September 13th, 1963. The idea was to build a 400 mph train capable of hovering over concrete hover tracks built a-top existing railways. A mock-up of the train, on which £10,000 had been spent in development, was demonstrated in secret to the Ministry of Transport and British Railways. Nothing came out of it and the project quietly died. Hovertrain is a generic term, and the vehicles are more commonly referred to by the projects that developed them in different countries – in the UK they are known as *tracked hovercraft*, in America as *tracked air-cushion vehicles*, and in France they are the *aerotrains*. News sources often conflate maglev trains with hovertrains, as both are levitated above the running surface, 'hovering' over them.

The cruellest cut of all, though, was the withdrawal of duty free services when the European Union removed tariffs between member states. Duty free sales had been the lucrative extra to bolster operational profits. Without that, the small margin of benefit over conventional cross-Channel ferry-boats was removed.

After 30 years in operation, the service finally closed in September 2000. It is said that the two Hovercraft were by this time thoroughly worn out and due for pensioning off.

Seaspeed also ran a service on the Solent linking Cowes and Southampton using passenger-only SR-N6 craft. This began in 1966 and was augmented soon afterwards by further routes from Ryde to Portsmouth and Portsmouth to Cowes. These routes were transferred to Hovertravel in 1976 and continue to this day.

Hovercraft Luddites

As long as there has been progress there's been a section of the general public for whom any advancement is unacceptable for one reason or another. Possibly no other part of the British Isles has incurred such wrath as Langstone Harbour yet I doubt if one in twenty could put a finger on it today!

Langstone lies in the Hampshire Flatlands of Portsmouth Harbour, Hayling Island and Havant. In 1935 there was a strident plan to develop the area as a vast land aerodrome and a huge seaplane port to replace Southampton. It was going to cost Portsmouth ratepayers half a million pounds which quickly rose to a million and a quarter and more and the subsidy zoomed up and down like a fiddler's elbow. It wasn't a good plan. Work began – and stopped with the outbreak of war.

In November 1962 there were new plans for Langstone which included a Hovercraft service. The Commodore of Eastney Cruising Association was a Mr. P J Parkhouse. 'If a hovercraft service was operated

There's three people in this Hovercraft… The second air-cushion vehicle to be built on the Isle of Wight was Britten-Norman's Cushioncraft. Piloted by Desmond Norman, Cushioncraft CC1 rides over the grass outside the hangar at Bembridge Airport in June 1960. Seated next to him are, left, Ron Benton, and to his right (in shirtsleeves), Peter Gattrell.

in Langstone Harbour, it would seriously interfere with cruising and sailing activities' he shouted at his Association's third annual dinner on November 21st.

John Mackett's otherwise commendable history of the passenger service between Ryde and Portsmouth (see Bibliography) is spoiled by a somewhat petulant account of recent times. 'In May 1959, a most unusual vehicle was wheeled out of the hanger [sic] of the Saunders, Roe Works [sic] in East Cowes. This was the… world's first all-metal hovercraft… it was two years before a craft capable of carrying passengers made its appearance. The following summer this craft operated another experimental service between Weston-Super-Mare and Cardiff.'

'In July 1965, Hovertravel Ltd started a regular services across Spithead using SR.N6 hovercraft, a development of the SR.N5 with seats for 38 passengers and a maximum speed of 64 knots over calm sea… In 1966 a limited summer service was started between Southsea and Sandown but it was not repeated in subsequent years.

'The Portsmouth Harbour-Ryde Pier Head hovercraft started in 1968, on April 1st; a date considered by many as being appropriate for the most erratic service ever to be seen on these waters! It used untried hovercraft of a different type and make from those used on other routes. The HM.2 built by Hovermarine Ltd of Southampton (now in liquidation) is an immersed-sidewall craft which is supported on an air cushion during flight but which is propelled through the water by conventional twin screws mounted on rigid side walls. It has the disadvantage of not being amphibious but the theoretical advantage of using marine diesel engines for both lifting and propulsion instead of the aircraft engines used on the SR.N6's.

'Everything possible has happened to this service!! The start was delayed by one week for 'technical modifications' and on the first day it was withdrawn from service for a time to untangle a rope from around its propellers, That same evening, it was returned to the makers for gearbox repairs. Later, it was withdrawn to have a skirt fitted. A second craft was acquired but it was not uncommon to find both out of action….'

Mr. Mackett continues in this unrelenting vein and sums up matters with a telling sentence: 'The crossing from Portsmouth or Southsea to Ryde by hovercraft is a boring business!' Mind you, one gets the feeling he'd say that about crossing the Channel, or travel from the Moon to Mars.

First trials of the Cushioncraft took place in the hangar and here it displayed its controllability problems. In spite of having the two propellers turning (in negative pitch for this trial), the craft could not 'hold station' and so here it is aided by John Britten, left, and Peter Gattrell, right. Desmond Norman is at the controls.

Finished and ready to be pushed outside, the Cushioncraft CC1 with designer John Britten standing in the foreground and Desmond Norman standing by the cockpit. It would still only travel in a circular fashion and much effort was devoted to producing fore-and-aft controlled travel.

The Hovercraft Fades from the Scene

The Hovercraft first appeared around 1953. By the start of the 21st century, its benefits had been exploited and, aside from a few specialist roles, it was a spent force. Half a century had seen the birth, development, exploitation and decline of the Hovercraft. What was left was just another means of transport for special applications, a piece of sporting fun for the young thrill-seeker – and a brief but fascinating history to record for future generations.

Crossing the Channel was no longer an adventure by sometimes rough-riding Hovercraft but could now be undertaken in absolute comfort by train and tunnel. If it was the Channel which had acted as a spur to the development and introduction of passenger and car transport Hovercraft, then it was the tunnel which quickly put them out of business.

Amateur Hovercraft Persist

With most things associated with developments in technology, it does not take too long for the amateur enthusiast to make his presence known. The world of Hovercraft shortened this lead-time considerably. One of the earliest amateur Hovercraft clubs was that formed at Brading on the Isle of Wight in about 1961-62 when a group successfully made and flew a free-ranging machine that traversed Brading Marshes.

This was the first of a number of such club activities that appeared up and down the land and rubbed development shoulders with the full-size Hovercraft engineers.

The Hovercraft represented one of the very small number of new technology opportunities where the amateur and the sophisticate actually level-pegged in the progress of development.

Principal Hovercraft Makers and Their History

British Hovercraft Corporation, East Cowes, Isle of Wight.
The British Hovercraft Corporation was the overall umbrella organisation created in March 1966 by the amalgamation of the three key participants in Hovercraft at that time – the Saunders-Roe division of Westland Aircraft (65%), Vickers Supermarine (25%), and the National Research Development Council (10%). The purpose was the creation of 'viable Hovercraft' for a world market.

It was a time of uncertain expansion which saw the rise and fall of a number of potentially significant makers such as Vickers, Denny and Land Rover and is characterised by an ever-growing trend towards seeking a possible justification rather than a valid purpose. By its very nature, BHC felt this more acutely than many other makers.

BHC will best be remembered as having painted the biggest Union Jack in the world on the doors of the one-time Saunders-Roe hangar at East Cowes to mark the Silver Jubilee of Queen Elizabeth in 1977. The doors stand 12m (39ft) tall and 46m (151ft) wide.

Britten-Norman Ltd/Cushioncraft Ltd, Bembridge Airport, Isle of Wight.
During the second half of 1949, two former De Havilland Technical College students, John Britten and Desmond Norman, started converting de Havilland Tiger Moths to operate as aerial crop-sprayers in the Sudan. This was to undertake contract work for banana growers Elders & Fyffe Ltd. Both men were resident on the Isle of Wight and John Britten's father was Island Magistrate while Desmond Norman's father had been one of the founders, in pre-war days, of Heston Aerodrome, West London.

Renting the one-time Labour Committee Rooms in Star Street, Ryde, the two young men began designing spray equipment conversions for the DH.82a Tiger Moth. Besides his work as magistrate, John Britten's father owned a chain of Island cinemas including Ryde's Commodore Cinema which backed on to the Star

The second Cushioncraft to be built, CC2 pictured here, was initially built without forward propulsion units or a skirt. Intended as an 11-passenger machine, the length was 30 feet and the beam 17 feet with power from a 240 hp Rolls-Royce LV.8 motor. The method of control and propulsion was originally air-jet deflection – a notoriously unreliable method when applied to the Hovercraft. Much later it would be modified and eventually acquire a skirt and two propeller-driving external engines for propulsion. In this posed publicity photograph, the entire workforce is pictured. The back row, standing, starts with Ronald Benton, fifth to the right is Peter Gattrell (principal craftsman in the team), centre of picture and at the extreme right, John Britten and Desmond Norman.

Street premises. With the backing of a friend Frank Herbert Mann, Forester Richard John Britten (1928-1977) and Nigel Desmond Norman (1929-2002) formed their first company, Britten-Norman Ltd in 1956.

As work in the French Cameroons and the Sudan increased they took over an existing firm called Crop Culture and formed a new business called Crop Culture (Aerial) Ltd with Jim McMahon as chief pilot and Jack Akers as manager. McMahon had also designed the dual-purpose hopper for the Tiger Moth which could be converted from solids (dusting) to liquids (spraying) very quickly. The operating company in the Sudan was a French-owned business called Ardic.

Back at Ryde, besides creating the necessary pumps and plumbing, Britten and Norman built Jim McMahon's chemical hopper and spray tanks which were located in the Moth's front cockpit position. They also took the existing Micronair rotary atomiser for dispersing chemicals and re-engineered it so that it could be applied to an aircraft: it was attached to a Tiger Moth wing-tip and rotated by a belt-driven adjustable fan. Much of this pioneering precision work was undertaken for them by Tim Hodges, owner of Ryde Model Shop who had a well-equipped workshop behind his retail outlet in the High Street.

During this period, Bembridge Airport was in the throes of sorting out a scandal of major proportions. The then Bembridge Flying Club was run by a gentleman named L K Holdaway and somebody had noticed certain light aircraft returning from week-ends in France doing a low pass over Bembridge's grass before high-tailing it to Southampton's Eastleigh Airport to clear Customs. And after the airfield fly-past people would be out on the airfield searching for something that might just have fallen from a low-flying Auster…

Britten-Norman's second air-cushion vehicle, the CC2, was rolled out of its workshop at Bembridge Airport in August 1961, making its first 'flight' on August 31st. It is seen here being inspected by newspaper men prior to a demonstration lift-off. The structure was so arranged that it could be broken down into three sections to facilitate transportation and packing. Unloaded it weighed about one and a half tons but was constructed to carry a payload equivalent to its own weight in cargo or passengers. Twelve passengers and their baggage was the load. Originally propelled by its single combined lift/propulsion engine, the machine underwent extensive modifications up to about six distinct versions. It also appeared with two flat four Continental engines mounted on pylons either side of the cabin. Because of a tendency to porpoise at speed, the hull was modified to provide a pronounced upturn at the front. This was the variant known as the CC3. While the later variants of the CC2 experimented with a skirt, the CC3 had no skirt and was merely an interim version leading up to the rather different CC4.

Came the morning when Customs & Excise decided to raid the airport, when they arrived at breakfast-time they found the place empty, deserted and abandoned. The flying club, the bar (and its supply of drinks) had all flown, together with Mr. Holdaway. It was widely reputed that he was tipped off about the forthcoming raid by the police…

It was a good year before the dust settled and Britten-Norman was able to move out of the cramped premises at Star Street into the little hangar at Bembridge Airport. This was the start of Britten-Norman's upwards spiral into success. Elders & Fyffe had long proclaimed a need for some sort of vehicle that could transport bananas out of plantations in the Southern Cameroons and when news of Christopher Cockerell's first Hovercraft reached the Isle of Wight, seeds of interest were sown over a wide area.

Over at Cowes, Maurice Joseph Brennan's pioneering Hovercraft, the SR.N1, was built and flown and very quickly John Britten was at work on his drawing-board with his own take on the Hovercraft with banana transport foremost in his mind. By 1960, the first B-N Hovercraft was ready for trials. They named it Cushioncraft and undertook initial trials on the airport while at the same time a fresh company, Cushioncraft Ltd, was registered as a division of Britten-Norman Ltd.

The board of Cushioncraft comprised F R J Britten, N Desmond Norman, J M McMahon and F H Mann (all directors of Britten-Norman), and Peter Winter (technical director). The business was reconstituted as a separate company (separate from B-N) in 1967 to permit British Hovercraft Corporation (BHC) to take a minority shareholding, and it revived the name under which Britten-Norman's initial air-cushion vehicle endeavours were launched. Anthony Rudolph Barrington Hobbs, BHC's nominee, now joined the board. With an authorised capital of £500,000 and issued capital of £450,000, BHC paid Britten-Norman £90,000 for a 20% stake in the firm's Hovercraft activities.

Renamed the Cushioncraft CC1, trials progressed with the prototype while the designers were at work on an even larger machine, the Cushioncraft CC2.

Eventually after many trials and much effort, the Isle of Wight pioneers settled on one design – the Cowes-based SR.N6 which was the first Hovercraft to be able to carry a 'coachload' of passengers. This was something of a watershed moment. One could relate to this as a volume rather the same way as news broadcasters describe the area of a battlefield, supermarket or disaster area in terms of 'football fields'. And a 'coachload' seemed an ideal load for the Isle of Wight/Portsmouth service.

The company evaluated the potential for the Cushioncraft in many countries and the result suggested the possibility of a transportation opportunity for air cushion vehicles which could accelerate the pace of development in those territories where roads were non-existent and fearsomely costly to build, and where rivers were seasonally unnavigable.

Although ultimately one of the country's most successful aircraft manufacturers, Britten-Norman was ever close to the wind and in 1971 it encountered financial problems. One outcome of this was that Cushioncraft Ltd was sold to the British Hovercraft Corporation in 1972 and the name disappeared.

The CC1 and early CC2 Cushioncraft were not provided with skirts and suffered from lack of directional control. The CC1 was prone to travel in a circular motion. In an attempt to control this, an overly large swept-back fin was fitted between the two propellers but this had very restricted effect. The CC2, several examples of which were built including models provided with two engines driving propellers as forward thrusters, was fitted with a skirt.

Cushioncraft Ltd, Bembridge, IoW, later Cowes, IoW.
Subsidiary of Britten-Norman Ltd [q.v.] sold off separately to the British Hovercraft Corporation in 1972.

William Denny & Brothers Ltd, Dumbarton, Scotland.
The old-established ship-building concern of Denny of Dumbarton entered the Hovercraft business in 1963 with a sidewall craft called the D1 which was transported by road for evaluation and trials which included

Townsend Car Ferries ran the Dover - Boulogne-sur-Mer cross-Channel service between 1968 and 1993 using all-passenger SR.N6 Hovercraft. This Hovercraft and Seacat service was opened in 1966 by Townsend Car Ferries. In 1993 Hoverspeed closed the Dover-Boulogne route after deciding that the Hoverport at Le Portel (near Boulogne-sur-Mer) was no longer required, and the SeaCat catamaran operation moved to nearby Folkestone. Hoverspeed was formed in 1981 by the merger of Seaspeed and Hoverlloyd. Here a bit of routine clearing is undertaken between trips. Note the life-raft storage in the upper spine behind the radar.

Loch Ness. Later the company experimented with the D2 Hoverlorry but this did little more than confirm the limitations of the non-beachable sidewall craft. Denny withdrew from Hovercraft.

Folland Aircraft Ltd, Sydney Lodge, Hamble, Southampton, Hampshire.

Founded as British Marine Aircraft Ltd in February, 1936, the business was reformed and renamed Folland Aircraft Ltd during 1937 with Henry Philip Folland (1889-1954) as managing director. Ill-health forced his retirement in 1951 and replacement by Westland Aircraft man William Edward Willoughby 'Teddy' Petter (1908-1968). In 1959 the business was absorbed into the Hawker Siddeley Group and the name Folland had been suppressed by 1963. In 1960, the one-time chief designer of Saunders-Roe, Maurice Joseph Brennan, moved to Follands and designed the prototype Ground Effect Research Machine (GERM) which marked Folland's first and only significant move into pure Hovercraft.

While the project was abandoned as a commercial venture, Brennan became fixated with the potential to convert surface-type vehicles into Hovercraft. Contemporary with Westland's soiree into designing trucks that were also helicopters, Brennan produced a number of schemes for military vehicles that could operate as Hovercraft. The company concluded that for the most difficult types of operation propulsion and manoeuvring forces called for power requirements equal in proportion to those required for lift. By comparison, operation over smoother surfaces offered considerable economies by employing surface contact in the form of immersed sidewalls and a marine propeller or water jet, or, for land operations, low-pressure tyres or tracks.

In the latter case the cushion could support most of the weight. Folland also evaluated various types of powerplant and for vehicle weights greater than about 70 tons it was concluded that gas turbines were essential. After practical experience with GERMs, possibly in remote parts of the world, the company

The workhorse of the ferry services was the small SR.N6 and here we see GH-2011 Britannia which was operated first by Townsend Ferries, then Cunard and finally Hoverwork. Townsend was the only operator to buy a new SR.N6 outright and began cross-Channel services from Dover Harbour in 1966 to a new hoverport at Calais which it shared with Hoverlloyd's own SR.N6 proving services. As Paine and Syme relate, after two months Townsend had only carried around 400 passengers as a result of weather and breakdowns (there were at least nine skirt failures). Now regular services were forgotten and the company ran sightseeing trips to Margate, Sheppey and then back to Dover and, on alternate days, Dungeness power station and Hastings. In 1967, the Hovercraft went on board the Cunarder *Sylvania* as a cruise experiment for the benefit of government officials along the Mediterranean shore. In 1968 Hovertravel bought it from Townsend for £37,500 less than they paid for it in 1966. Here it is pictured on Hastings Beach.

Meanwhile, Britten-Norman had moved on with its Cushioncraft and the latest CC4, seen here, was the outcome of joint design work between the Hovercraft Development Ltd and the Bembridge-based company. It was proposed as the first small Hovercraft for production but this never happened. A six-seater, it was 24 feet 3 inches in length and 13 feet 9 inches wide, power being provided by a 240 hp Rolls-Royce LV8 engine. As can be seen in this view, this was the first example to be fitted with a primitive form of skirt. In this 1964 photograph can be seen Cushioncraft 'test-pilot' Peter Ayles and Christopher Bland. Bland went on to become managing director of Hovertravel and Air Vehicles Limited (two other Britten-Norman companies) and became Lord Lieutenant of the Isle of Wight (1995-2008).

---

proposed a series of commercial vehicles. The first Hovertruck would carry five tons of freight at up to 30 m.p.h. over land or reasonably smooth water. Future Hovercoaches were envisaged for amphibious operation, carrying 20 tons or 150 passengers at 80 knots, and having a range of 600 nautical miles. At a 1962 military exhibition Folland unveiled eight different types of vehicle, displaying large models in a realistic model terrain. Military chiefs at home and abroad showed mild interest but the project was dropped. Folland briefly pursued other Hovercraft projects such as the hover-stretcher which was designed in collaboration with the Army Medical Corps.

Griffon Hoverwork Ltd, Woolston, Southampton, Hampshire.
Griffon Hoverwork claims a long history of involvement in the Hovercraft Industry. The unnamed founders of the business say that they set up the world's first Hovercraft operation, alongside Sir Christopher Cockerell and this business (Hovertravel) continues to flourish as part of the Bland Group. Some of this experience seems to go back to the developmental days of the British Hovercraft Corporation, knowledge and experience now applied in new product development today. The company, which says it was born out of the acquisition and merger of Griffon Hovercraft and Hoverwork by the Bland Group in 2008, uniting almost half a century of Hovercraft design, manufacture and operational experience, is also the design authority for the original and subsequent British Hovercraft Corporation designs.

Saunders-Roe (SARO Ltd) Ltd, Columbine Works, Cowes, Isle of Wight.
One of the oldest businesses in the area, the boat-building business of Sam Saunders came into its own when it was taken over by A V Roe and Saunders-Roe Ltd in 1929. It then expanded into aircraft, flying boats and seaplane construction, making the first Hovercraft (in the world as it turned out) as the SR.N1 in 1965

This company also collaborated with The National Research & Development Corporation in Hovercraft design and development until it then founded The British Hovercraft Co using the same premises on the Cowes waterfront.

With the formation of new manufacturing and design companies, firms such as Saunders-Roe, Westland and Cushioncraft fell by the wayside, either bought out and amalgamated, or effectively put out of business. Descended from Saunders-Roe and Westland, although perhaps not showing it, the British Hovercraft Corporation's BH-7 *Wellington* Hovercraft, XW255 is seen on trials off the South Coast. It was a practical-looking vessel which saw military service in Iran and Saudi Arabia.

Vickers-Armstrong Ltd, South Marston Works, Swindon, Wiltshire.

The old-established aircraft makers Vickers-Armstrong watched with interest as Saunders-Roe experimented with its SR.N1 in the latter part of 1959 and then decided that its South Marston Works, near Swindon, should be turned over, in part at least to Hovercraft production. In November 1959, and just before the firm's extensive aircraft interests were transferred to the British Aircraft Corporation, it successfully negotiated a licence to manufacture a prototype from the Hovercraft Development Corporation. The company actively entered the Hovercraft field in 1961. Besides the Swindon works, the firm also maintained a trials base on the River Itchen, Southampton. Four craft were developed (the VA-1, VA-2, VA-3, VA-3A and the Hover Rover) and a fifth (VA-4) was proposed as a concept which was very similar to the original Westland's SR-N4 concept. In 1966 the Vickers' and Westland's Hovercraft activities were merged to form the British Hovercraft Corporation (shareholdings – Westland Aircraft 65%, Vickers 25%, National Research and Development Corporation 10%) – the Westland's designs continued, the Vickers' designs did not. By 1971, Westland Aircraft had bought out both of the other partners and Vickers' connection with Hovercraft was at an end.

Test pilot for the scheme was Leslie Robert Colquhoun (1921-2001) who had made a name for himself (as well as securing a well-earned George Medal) by successfully landing an Attacker jet fighter with one wing folded.

Vickers' first Hovercraft was the VA-1, a rather basic and small model built in the main from resin-bonded plywood and which lifted itself up on a narrow peripheral wall of air claimed to require less power and produce less slipstream.

Two further machines – VA-2 and a much larger VA-3 – were made but overall there seems to have been some relief when the firm finally closed its Hovercraft activities.

The South Marston works is now a car production site for Honda.

Vosper-Thorneycroft Ltd, Portsmouth, Hampshire.

Vosper was established as early at 1871 by Herbert Edward Vosper as a repairer and refitter of ships for the Navy. Later Vosper would become associated with the design and manufacture of Motor Torpedo boats and Moor Gun boats for the Royal Navy in the Second World War. During the 1960 the company moved into larger vessels for other than home-consumption. It was now that the company's size became a crucial issue and so, in 1966, it merged with John Isaac Thorneycroft & Company.

In 1965 Vosper decided to enter the Hovercraft business and applied to the NRDC, technology licensees, for permission to build the VT-1 described as 'a semi-amphibious craft with underwater propellers'. This was finally launched in prototype form during 1969.

Two production VT-1 vessels followed but they were not particularly successful and were scrapped in 1973. An 'improved' version, the VT-2, was sold to the IHTU but when that facility folded in 1981, it was sold for scrap. This marked the end of Vosper-Thorneycroft's short and unsuccessful soiree into Hovercraft.

Westland Aircraft Ltd, Yeovil, Somerset, and Cowes, IoW.

Westland Aircraft Ltd was an old-established West Country aircraft manufacturer formed as a separate company by Petters Ltd just before the outbreak of the First World War. After the Second World War, Westlands secured a licence first for the manufacture an American-designed helicopter in Yeovil and, later, was able to design and produce an improved all-British version of it.

Westland Aircraft took over Saunders-Roe late in 1959. Between then and 1961 the British government forced the consolidation of 20 or so British aviation firms into three larger groups with the threat of withheld contracts and the lure of project funding. While the majority of fixed-wing aircraft design and construction lay with the British Aircraft Corporation and the Hawker Siddeley Group, the helicopter divisions of Bristol, Fairey and Saunders-Roe (with their Hovercraft) were merged with Westland to form Westland Helicopters in 1961.

Along the way there had been successes and failures as designs had fallen by the wayside. One of the formative designs that remained in circulation for research and development use for a long while was the one and only Westland SR.N2 seen here undergoing mixed-terrain trials in Canada in 1961.

Although only one was ever built, the SR.N2 can be regarded as the prototype for subsequent commercial Hovercraft which followed on from the somewhat primitive SR.N1 research craft. It was demonstrated on the Saint Lawrence River, Canada in 1962 and operated as a ferry on the River Severn in 1963. It was then fitted with deeper (4 feet) skirts to improve its performance in rough seas. Southdown Motor Services and Westland Aircraft operated the SR.N2 on the Solent between Eastney and Ryde in 1963/4, carrying a massive 30,000 passengers. Job done, it was eventually broken up.

British Hovercraft Corporation was the corporate entity created when the Saunders-Roe division of Westland Aircraft and Vickers Supermarine combined in March 1966 with the intention of creating viable commercial Hovercraft.

None of the Vickers designs were 'taken forward', the existing production of the Saunders-Roe designs continued (SR.N5 *Warden* Class and SR.N6 *Winchester* Class) and the Saunders-Roe-designed *Mountbatten* Class Hovercraft (SR.N4), was completed and entered the cross-Channel service.

Only one new design was produced (1969) by the British Hovercraft Corporation, the BH.7 known as the *Wellington* Class.

In 1970, Westland Aircraft acquired the shares of the other parties and the following year acquired the Cushioncraft company from Britten-Norman.

In 1984 the company name was changed to Westland Aerospace – Hovercraft design/manufacture had effectively ceased and the company was involved with the manufacture of composite materials for the Aerospace industry.

Other applications of Hovercraft technology

The principles that have given mankind the successful Hovercraft have been shown to offer more than mere advantages of transportation. These extend from moving damaged or crashed aircraft without causing further damage, shifting a heavy concert pipe organ over a sprung maple dance-floor and a simple tool for mowing the domestic garden lawn.

Luck-pushing at its best! The SR.N5 being encouraged to traverse some pretty improbable terrain for the benefit of the PR-man's camera. One is encouraged to suggest that it's amazing the difference a bit of skirt makes, except that this manoeuvre is being undertaken at some speed.

A Swedish inventor named Karl Dahlman saw Christopher Cockerell's Hovercraft and thus inspired invented the first hover-mower in 1964. It was blue in colour and was named the Flymo, a brand name registered to the Swedish company Husqvarna AB, formerly a part of Electrolux. The mower was a variation of the conventional petrol powered rotary push lawn mower having a fan above the mower's spinning blades to create a downward stream of air as it turned. This lifted the whole mower off the grass so that it floated, making it very easy to push around the lawn. Exhibited at the 1964 Brussels Inventors Fair, it won its inventor the gold medal at first showing. In the space of a very short while, the hover mower became so familiar to the modern gardener that it may be hard to accept that the first Flymo produced was as recently as 1965 and was powered by a small petrol engine. The first all-electric one came four years later. Its familiar orange colour of today only dates back to 1977.

Aircraft recovery is an ever-present problem at major airports. If an aircraft suffers undercarriage problems or simply veers off the runway onto soft ground, it creates a blockage in the free-flowing operation of the airfield. Unless it can be moved quickly and safely, the airfield has to shut down with consequent disruption to travel plans and movements. Two Southampton companies addressed this problem in 1970 and came up with inflatable air bags attached to 'hover-platforms', with which an aircraft can be lifted and then moved away on a cushion of air with both ease and safety. Now equipment is provided at all the world's main airports so that if an emergency should arise, the incapacitated aircraft can be moved with a 'Hovercraft trailer' in double-quick time.

In Adelaide's Festival Centre, South Australia, is a concert pipe organ known locally as 'the world's only musical Hovercraft'. Commissioned in 1978 to mark Queen Elizabeth II's Silver Jubilee, the $430,000 organ, has 4,250 pipes and was built by the world-famous Austrian maker, Rieger Orgelbau. Besides being one of the biggest in South Australia, it possesses one unique feature: it can be moved by one person on a cushion of air.

The Festival Centre is used for a wide variety of entertainments, organ concerts being just one. To facilitate this 'multi-tasking', the organ stands at the back of the stage when not in use and is brought forward when it is itself the star performer. Because the front stage is also a sprung dance-floor, it was not possible to roll the organ into position on wheels, so the huge instrument is floated on a cushion of air controlled by one operator.

Other applications have included experimental hover-trains – a French invention – and hovering lorries which can truck heavy goods across unsuitable terrain.

Accidents and Mishaps

In view of the very many services that have been initiated by Hovercraft around the world and in consideration of the experimental nature of many of these operations, it is perhaps remarkable that there have been very few accidents or incidents. Indeed Hovercraft operation appears to have maintained a fairly anodyne history. Of course there was, certainly in the early days of public service, freak gusts of wind and waves which tore or otherwise damaged the Hovercraft's skirt and there was one celebrated occasion when a *Mountbatten* Class cross-Channel vessel was entering Dover Harbour in violent weather conditions which dashed the bows against the harbour wall and did rather a lot of structural damage and caused minor injuries to some passengers.

But finally real tragedy struck with an accompanying loss of life. And this wasn't even in the rough water of a Channel crossing but in the usually placid waters of the Ryde-Portsmouth passenger service. It would go down as the world's first fatal accident involving a commercially-operated Hovercraft.

At the other end of the scale, Hovercraft offered a great sporting opportunity as demonstrated by this skirtless flying motorcycle which was made by students at America's Princeton University's Department of Aero Engineering. More of a 'concept vehicle' than a prototype, the 1961 vehicle was powered by a 7 hp Nelson engine provided with a recoil starter. It was actually evaluated by the US Army.

It was the afternoon of Saturday, March 4th, 1972, when the Portsmouth-bound SR.N6 overturned in a gale 400 yards off Southsea shore. Five people were killed but a million-to-one chance saved the lives of 22 others who were rescued either from the sea or the inverted hull of the cross-Solent vessel.

The officer-in-chief of the Eastney Auxiliary Coastguard Station, John Andrews, just happened to be in his car in a seafront car park when he saw the Hovercraft flip up and over. Later Andrews told in detail what happened next:

'I immediately radioed for all assistance, the helicopters from RAF Thorney Island, lifeboats and inshore rescue craft,' he said. 'There was a strong tide ebbing across the Hamilton Banks and it was a freak of tide, wave and wind that capsized her. She tilted half down and then went over. In all the years I have been here I have never seen such a freak of conditions,' he added.

For the survivors waiting on the upturned hull, Mr. Andrews's instant call for help meant the difference between life and death. Meanwhile hundreds of onlookers who had gathered around the Hovertravel terminal at Clarence Pier, quickly realised the full horror of the tragedy when a woman's body was winched out of the sea by helicopter and carried over the heads of the crowd on the beach to be landed near a waiting ambulance on Southsea Common.

Two other bodies were then brought ashore by pilot boat. 'Several people meeting friends and relations on the Hovercraft waited in an agony of suspense to see if they too would be among the dead,' reported the local newspaper.

Claimants to be alternative Hovercraft pioneers include a country doctor in America named Bertelsen. 38-year-old William R Bertelsen was resident medic in the 500-strong township of Neponset, Illinois. He was concerned at the rugged terrain needed to be traversed in order to visit his outer-most patients, so he thought up an air-cushion 'car' which he named the Aeromobile. The vehicle that Bertlesen first built in or around 1959 was a conventional skirtless plenum-chamber vehicle. This was his second attempt and offered more creature comforts than his prototype. The vehicle was never put into production.

A regular user of the Hovercraft service was 29-year old Hugh Lake from Westbourne, near Emsworth. He stated that: 'it happened so quickly. We were approaching the beach at Southsea and were just passing the approach channel to the harbour. A big sea was running straight down the Solent and the wind was making the waves steep. All I can think of is that a couple of waves broke over the port side and another wave lifted the craft.'

Those that died were two from Portsmouth, one from Rogate, West Sussex, and a husband and wife from Surrey. The upshot of this accident was a rule that all Hovercraft drivers should henceforth wear seat-belts.

On a later occasion, and in dense fog, despite carrying radar, the Hovertravel Hovercraft collided head-on at speed with the ordinary British Railways Isle of Wight ferry. It was November 2nd, 1972, and the sound of the heavy impact caused consternation on shore. Miraculously, nobody was injured which was fortuitous: on board for the trip was Sir Matthew Slattery, then Chairman of the Air Registration Board.

There has been the occasional misdemeanor including a recent one which, incidentally, brought to the forefront once more the old argument 'what is a Hovercraft?' It was a June day in 2014 when Hovertravel's SR.N6, GH-2035, set off on its usual Portsmouth-Isle of Wight run. The Hovercraft got to Ryde and had great difficulty beaching so much so that a relief pilot had to get aboard and bring the vessel ashore. The cause of the problem? Apparently the pilot was drunk and found to have 96 microgrammes of alcohol in 100ml of breath – almost three times the legal limit.

Charged in Court in Cowes under the Railways and Transport Safety Act, 2003, there was initial confusion among police and prosecutors as to whether, under the Act, a Hovercraft counted as a ship or as a flying

Roll-out day at Columbine Works, Cowes. The famous doors which once read 'Saunders-Roe', later 'Westland Aircraft Ltd' and now 'British Hovercraft Corporation' reveal that the SR.N4 (now spelled without its median full-stop) was about the largest vessel it was possible to construct in the historic flying-boat hangar on the River Medina. It wasn't called 'the World's largest Hovercraft' for nothing! The picture dates from 1967.

machine. His charge-sheet had to be amended but when the 50-year-old pilot with 20 years' experience as a Hovercraft pilot was sentenced, his hovering days were clearly at an end.

Finally, time to come clean with a story from the very early days of hovering about. I happened to be riding an experimental sortie as co-pilot in one of the early Hovercraft driven by a senior Saro captain-flyer together with a close pal from Sandown Airport. It was very much a case of trying to tame a vessel which was, by all accounts, unsteerable and we were making various vectored approaches to the beach to find the best way of beaching our craft in a fitful wind. We were uncomfortably close to a small moored rowing-boat in the shallows in the lee of Ryde Pier. The more we tried to steer away from the little wooden boat the closer we got until the inevitable happened – and we sat ourselves down firmly on top of it. As we rose from our demonstration of poor hovermanship, we could clearly see the boat beneath us sitting on the bottom – in about four feet of water. One of us clambered out and grabbed the mooring rope from the floating buoy and with difficulty heaved the sunken craft to the surface. We turned it upside down and shook all the water out of it before very gently putting it back in the water – whereupon it went Glug! Glug! and quickly sank back to the sand without even a show of bubbles. Unfortunately we had managed to spring every joint in its little hull. We opened up the Hovercraft and beat a hasty if hesitant retreat… A hard thing to achieve with the correct degree of aplomb when myriads of curious shoreborne eyes are watching a new craft on test.

The Story in Pictures

It's a bit sobering having lived through the lifespan of a technological shift and seen what has come out 'the other side' meaning what is left of it all. We were all so bright-eyed and bushy-tailed back in the 1950s when it all started. There's still some Hovercraft out there doing good stuff including a fragile service to the Isle of Wight where I lived for many years before and after the war.

In this collection are pictures which I think you will find interesting for various reasons. Many are mine, others taken by friends and some by professionals. I hope I have chosen them well enough to please you

If the SR.N6 was the Jack-o'-all-trades runabout for the Hovercraft, the much larger SR.N4 was the cross-Channel behemoth. These were truly enormous vessels. Here we see the Mk.2 model which included *The Princess Margaret* and *The Princess Anne*, both seen here at the Ramsgate cross-Channel terminal. Their sheer size is something to behold.

Memorials traditionally remember the sad ending of something much loved. Nowhere is this more poignantly demonstrated than on the now-abandoned hard at Dover where this solitary propeller and its steerable support marks all that remains of the once-great Hoverspeed/Hoverlloyd ferry terminal. Few could have realised that the Hovercraft would endure in commercial service less than 30 years after which it would be relegated to museum and history books.

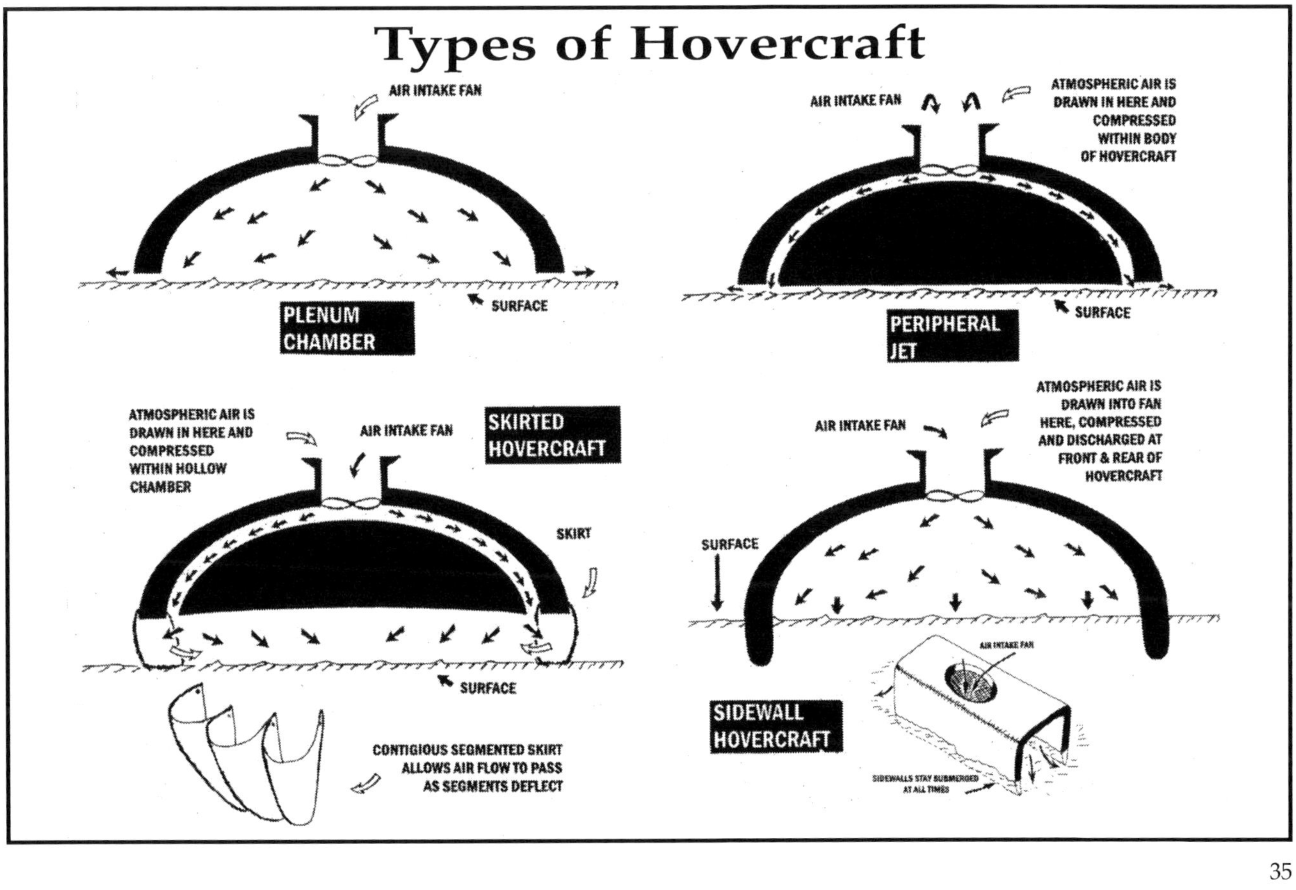

The man accredited with the invention of the Hovercraft is Christopher Cockerell (1910-1999). He was knighted in 1969 for his work in engineering. Cambridge-born, Cockerell's father was curator of the Fitzwilliam Museum. Following his interest in engineering and ship-building, it was in an attempt to minimise hull drag that Christopher Cockerell conceived the idea of the lifting air cushion and, by 1955, he had a working model. Three years later, having attracted the interest and support of the National Research Development Corporation, the first full-size Hovercraft was ordered from Saunders-Roe on the Isle of Wight and in January the following year, the NRDC formed a dedicated subsidiary called The Hovercraft Development Ltd. Cockerell was appointed Technical Director and the company controlled the patents which it used to license several private sector firms to manufacture craft under the registered trademark of Hovercraft. Here is Sir Christopher Cockerell with his model air cushion vehicle.

Remembered as a man of humour and humanity – Christopher Cockerell in his boat-building days. Cockerell received the CBE in 1966 and was knighted in 1999.

The SR.N1 was a vast leap into the unknown for Saunders-Roe and despite the steep learning curve, the craft was at the forefront of development for almost three years during which times its essentially circular planform was repeatedly revised and various forward power units tried out. This vessel never carried a skirt. Note the 'B' Class aircraft registration G-12-4. That so much experimental work could be carried out with the SR.N1 was a tribute to its overall flexibility of design and it was only really advances in skirt technology and in underskirt labyrinths that finally rendered the machine obsolete.

Initially circular in planform, the provision of tall fins was of little aid to proceeding in a straight line and the hull was continually tweaked to improve yaw control. If the SR.N1 was the prototype working Hovercraft, then we certainly had our moneys'-worth out of it. It was revised many times over from the Mk.11, 111, 1V models. It was discovered early on that the 435 hp simply wasn't powerful enough to provide both propulsion and lift since it generated no more than a speed of 25 knots and a clearance or hull depth of no more than eight or nine inches. A second engine was installed for forward propulsion, this being a Bristol Siddeley Viper gas turbine. The increase in performance was quite remarkable despite the fact that the new engine was twice as heavy as the prototype. A speed of 70 knots was now achievable. The hover height was now increased to more than a foot.

The world's second air-cushion vehicle also hailed from the Isle of Wight, this time the young and still unknown firm of Britten-Norman. In this picture of the first Cushioncraft, Desmond Norman stands by the cabin door with John Britten in the foreground. The motor-car wheel and tyre which drove the peripheral fan can also be seen. It was this system of creating lift that made the CC1 singularly quiet – a feature unfortunately lost with subsequent Hovercraft types. Its circular shape and lack of visible controls contributed to a delightfully random method of flight and all ascents had to be accompanied by a number of people standing around the periphery guiding the machine. On its second flight it flew into an area of rough grass and required the use of a crane to be lifted back to the hangar's concrete standing. In 1961, CC1 went to the Inter-Service Hovercraft Trials unit. Soon afterwards withdrawn from use, it was presented to the Royal Military College of Science.

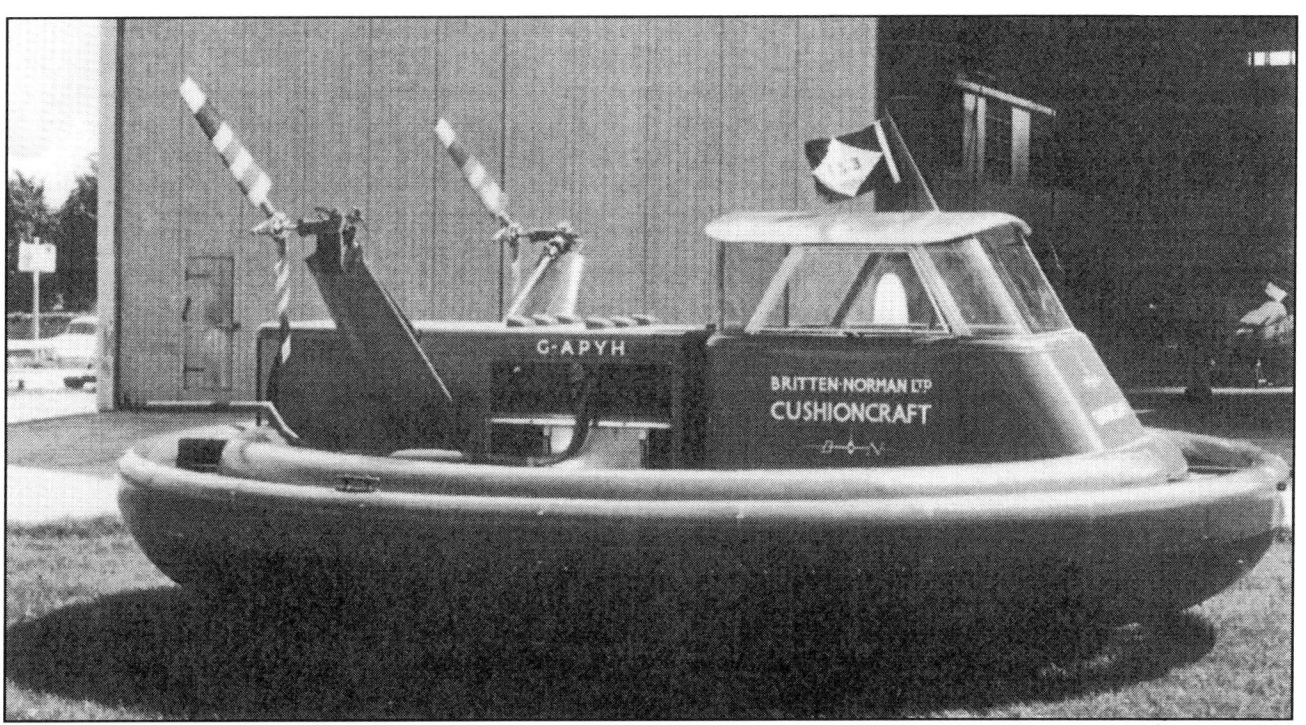

Designed and built during 1959 and 1960, the Britten-Norman Cushioncraft was the second Hovercraft to fly, its first lift-off taking place on June 21st 1960. The twin rotors were actually Hiller helicopter tail rotors.

Uncertain as those days were, the Cushioncraft was considered more akin to an aircraft than a boat or any other type of vehicle so it was allocated the civil aircraft registration G-APYH on February 9th 1960. Some 18 feet 10 inches in diameter, it weighed one ton and had a 40-blade lifting fan built into the peripheral decking and driven by a 160 hp Coventry Climax engine. Having no skirt, its maximum altitude on smooth concrete was between 12 and 15 inches.

The Britten-Norman CC1 Cushioncraft prototype pictured on its press-day launch in June 1960 at Bembridge Airport on the Isle of Wight. John Britten and Desmond Norman stand together behind the open cockpit door. The CC1 was built before skirt technology and while able to achieve at height of 12 to 15 inches, directional control was very much a hit and miss affair. After many modifications, the last one was to fit the CC1 with a single very large swept-back fin. Because the craft was essentially circular, the additional side area had too little moment to provide much in the way of yaw control. Shortcomings aside, the Cushioncraft was a successful air cushion vehicle (ACV) built and flown in Britain.

Experimental Cushioncraft CC1 suffered from the understandable problems that there was nothing in its geometry that would keep it straight, let alone make it responsibly steerable. Finally a fixed fin with movable rudder was installed. As hindsight proves, this was a non-effective solution since the fin and rudder needed to be considerably further aft in order to be effective. This was the swansong for the CC1 as the CC2 emerged to take over as an upgraded research vessel.

Bearing the civil aircraft registration G-ARSM, Cushioncraft CC2 was only slightly more controllable than the CC1 and was steered and propelled by air deflection within the cushion. This one prototype model would undergo a number of design changes and modifications over the years.

Britten-Norman's Cushioncraft CC2 was designed for amphibious operations. Like the SR.N1 at Cowes it was skirtless and consequently had a maximum ground clearance of twelve inches and a maximum speed of 40 mph. It could seat twelve passengers plus one driver and travel at up to 40 mph.

Britten-Norman's Cushioncraft CC4 Hovercraft was the result of collaboration with the Hovercraft Development Ltd. It was equipped with a skirt from the beginning. Of all the Hovercraft made, though, this had by far the largest proportion of its hull skirted and, despite being pocket-pleated at the bottom, it proved less than durable. Furthermore, the skirt problems had been foreseen and the covering was in sections – only these leaked far more severely than planned. Aside from that, the CC4 was a better vessel than the earlier ones and could be driven easily in a straight line. It saw out its days with the National Physical Laboratory which reclassified it as HU-4.

The fifth Cushioncraft, the CC5, marked the progressive development of the previous models, especially the CC4. With a length of 29 feet and a beam of 15 feet 6 inches, this was a six/eight seater powered by a 240 hp Rolls-Royce LV 841 engine driving four centrifugal fans each 3 feet 6 inches in diameter providing both lift and propulsion. Whereas the fans on the CC4 were widely spaced because the engine was installed between each side pair, the CC5 had them closer together because the engine was no longer between them. Another major difference was that while the earlier machine's four fans combined to produce lift and propulsion, the CC5 divided these duties, the front two fans being responsible for lift while the aft pair provided motive power. Each of the two rear jet orifices was flanked by a pair of rudders and a pair of pitch-trim surfaces to regulate and control the roll and wallow behaviour. These surfaces were interlinked, providing the driver with a wide range of combinations to control the stability of the craft. On top of this, the jet thrust could be reversed to provide braking. The hull comprised a number of watertight buoyancy chambers, each with an individual inspection hatch and with it a mechanism for pumping it dry in the event of water ingress. Only one example of this model was built and it first hovered in March 1966. Trials were undertaken in Priory Bay between Nettlestone and Bembridge Harbour but in October that year it suddenly capsized and, although salvaged, was scrapped.

A little-remembered Hovercraft was the Air Cushion Developments Ltd's ACD-1, a skirtless machine which was the product of a small company at Dibden Purliue, Hampshire. Described in *Flight* (June 28th, 1962) as 'an entirely new British air cushion vehicle', this machine distinguished itself by carrying the British Prime Minister, Harold Macmillan (he of 'the night of the Long Knives') on its first tethered flight trials which took place at Luton Hoo on June 23rd. The craft was powered by one Gipsy Queen 32 engine which drove four fans for lift and propulsion. These were manufactured at Weybridge by The Airscrew Company & Jicwood Ltd. At a weight in excess of four long tons, the Hovercraft managed to attain a height of approximately 18 inches. The two men standing on the deck appear to pose an interesting body-language scenario…

Vickers Armstrong entered the Hovercraft field in 1961 with three main models (VA-1, 2 and 3) plus a hoverised Land Rover and a fourth (the VA-4) was proposed as a concept. This was rather similar to the Westland SR.N4. Here is a good overall view of the VA-1 which was constructed primarily from resin-bonded plywood. The aircraft 'B' Class markings G-15-252 are, in fact, those of Supermarine.

Vickers VA-1 in the hover showing approximately 18 inches of clear air beneath the skirtless craft.

Vickers VA-1, G-15-252, first appeared without a forward cabin. Made mainly out of resin-bonded plywood, the VA-1 was 35 feet long and 13 feet wide and power was provided, unusually, by two different aircraft engines – a 139 hp Gipsy Major for lift and a 133 hp AVCO Continental CF.90 for propulsion. Sea trials were undertaken at the manufacturers' Itchen Works near Southampton and as seen here a detachable front cabin was fitted.

Vickers' last Hovercraft was the 12-ton VA-3. It made its first hover at South Marston on March 25th, 1962 and began its sea trials in April 1962. It had fins at the front and rear and no skirt. Unlike the Saunders-Roe vessel, it had separate engines for lift and propulsion. Length was 54 feet 9 inches and beam 27 feet. It could carry 24 passengers at 60 knots and was powered by four 425 hp Bristol Siddeley gas turbines – two each for lift and propulsion. On July 20th, 1962, the VA-3 began an experimental 'proving service' across the Dee Estuary between Ryhl and Wallasey's Moreton Beach, pictured here. In February 1964, the VA-3 went to America for trials with the US Navy: it returned to Southampton in May, 1965.

On its way to the Dee Estuary for practical passenger trials, the Vickers VA-3 is hoisted aboard a ship at Southampton for the journey.

Operator British United Airways with the Vickers VA-3 Hovercraft on Moreton Beach during the experimental service between Wallasey and Ryhl in the summer of 1962.

Hovercraft seemed to spend much of their early life going somewhere else to participate in trials beyond the apparent range of their hovering ability. This is why there are so many pictures of Hovercraft hanging in the air above boats. It also allows a detailed view of the skirts, where fitted. Here the Vickers VA-3 is seen being loaded onto a vessel at Southampton in 1954. This machine was fitted with a relatively shallow skirt of high-aspect-ratio fingers which, had the craft undergone more development work, would have been expected to have been upgraded to one with stiffer fingers.

Vickers VA-3 was developed in 1962 and went on to operate the world's first Hovercraft passenger service. With a passenger capacity of 24, the vessel ran six services a day and even carried Royal Mail so creating the world's first Hovercraft mail service as well. Although it was to prove popular, unreliable engines and bad weather were factors leading to the service only running for 36 days out of a 59-day scheduled trials period. The VA-3, like the SR.N1, had no skirt and thus had a limited hover height, so restricting its operation to none but the calmest of days. The VA-3 001's passenger use ended on 17th September, 1962 during extreme weather, when breaking loose from her moorings she had to be towed ashore by Rhyl Lifeboat, however not before extreme damage had been done to the structure, rendering her unfit for further passenger service. The picture shows the craft being refuelled.

In the colours of British United Airways, Vickers Hovercraft VA-3. G-15-253, operated the world's first Hovercraft passenger service between Ryhl and Wallasey, Cheshire, in 1962. This publicity photographs advises that the craft had a cruising speed of 60 mph and a 'weight capacity' of two tons with a carrying capacity of 24 passengers and one traffic officer.

Off the shore at Lee-on-Solent, the Vickers VA-3 demonstrates its high-speed capabilities. Built and developed in 1962, soon after the SR.N1 proved the Hovercraft concept viable, after trials in the Solent, British United Airways operated the VA-3 on the first ever passenger route across the estuary of the River Dee between Rhyl, North Wales and Moreton Beach, near Liverpool.

The Vickers hovering hovertruck, a Land Rover-based Hovercraft of 1962. Used for crop-spraying, the spray-booms are pivoted at the front grille. In 1962 two new technologies were in the ascendency – Hovercraft and aerial crop-spraying. Vickers-Armstrong took a Land Rover and turned it into a Hover Rover for agricultural spraying duties. What one calls a 'four-by-four' that also flies has so far not been determined. In this view the spray booms are folded back and secured to the bodywork.

A converted Series II 109 pick-up, the Hover Rover was developed to minimise ground-pressure, allowing the traversing of boggy ground. However, it suffered a problem in that it needed two engines. Besides that of the normal Land Rover, the establishment of the hover air required a second motor. Never intended as a commercial venture the Hover Rover appeared at several demonstrations presumably to keep the Vickers name in the news. Vickers went on to build the 24-passenger VA-3 which looked a lot less like a lash-up.

Vickers VA-1 Hoverjeep – an idea that seemed to be seeking an opportunity. The concept, while interesting, was evaluated by the British Army at Larkhill, Wiltshire, in 1963, but was never put into production.

A British Army display with a hovering Land Rover on demonstration at Chertsey in 1962. With the vehicles propensity for coping with most terrains, the purpose of the conversion was a little uncertain but, whatever it was, it must have been impressive…

While Hovercraft were suited to many roles, not all were either as practical or so attractive. These craft invariably 'self selected' their own duties and occupations and one of these was the catamaran. Clearly nothing to do with the pure Hovercraft, it nevertheless had a useful role to play in ferry services and was akin to a sidewall craft. The Portsmouth-Ryde ferry was for some time operated by catamarans, being both fast and reliable while being more or less free from incidental damage. It also found favour on other ferry routes. Here the Hoverspeed SeaCat *Great Britain* departs Douglas, Isle of Man.

One of the lesser-known companies engaged in developing Hovercraft in the second half of 1961 was Folland. Alongside Saunders-Roe (which became Westland), Vickers and Britten-Norman (Cushioncraft), Folland was working on its own solution (a large machine called the Folland Hovertruck) until in 1959 it was acquired by Hawker Siddeley which had dropped the Folland name by 1963. Saunders-Roe's Hovercraft chief designer Maurice Joseph Brennan (who designed the SR.N1) left in 1959 to join Folland. Here he worked on Folland's Ground Effect Research Vehicle or GERM, pictured here on March 20th 1961. Piloted by John Chaplin, Folland's chief Hovercraft development engineer, the machine was demonstrated at Imphal Barracks, York, where it hovered three inches about the ground. The craft was powered by a pair of 700 cc Royal Enfield motorcycle engines.

Maurice J Brennan had been chief designer for Saunders-Roe but in the early part of 1959 he moved over to Folland at Hamble and there worked upon the prototype GERM or Ground Effect Research Machine. It first flew under Folland's 'B' Conditions registration, G-39-15. Although it was abandoned as a commercial venture, the GERM encouraged Henry Folland to explore other Hovercraft applications including the hover-stretcher which was designed in conjunction with the Army Medical Corps.

Hovercraft Development Ltd's HD1-001 at Cowes in 1963. It appeared with a variety of minor modifications, in particular as in regard to number and position of the fins and rudders.

While air-cushion technology had developed by the end of the 1970s, there were still problems for the Hovercraft which had not completely been addressed. By now companies had been established in various parts of the world to manufacture Air Cushion Vehicles of all sizes from recreational vessels to practical ferries. Many of these companies did not last particularly long. There was a general belief that Hovercraft were fine examples of that genus – a solution looking for a problem. Trial passenger services gained a reputation for unreliability and short lived operation. Only the established services across the Solent and the Channel proved viable in the long term. One of these was Hovermarine which built a prototype, completed in 1968 and operated by Seaspeed between Ryde Pier Head and Portsmouth Harbour. This, the HM-2, also operated the Hovercat service built up by the Manx Hovercat Co. A small firm had been formed in 1965 called Hovermarine to build sidewall Hovercraft ferries and this was licensed by the Hovercraft Development Ltd in 1967. The factory was at Woolston, Southampton, where sidewall and Hovercat Hovercraft were manufactured initially. This factory was destroyed by fire in February 1969 as a result of which the firm went into voluntary liquidation and the assets acquired by a new company, Hovermarine Transport Ltd, which was subsequently taken over by the American firm, Transportation Technology, Inc. Subsequent production of a variant as the HD-221 fireboat saw the vessel with a small US market centred on the firm's US factory at Titusville in Florida. In early 1980 the Vosper Group purchased 51% of the company which had been a wholly owned subsidiary of the Hovermarine Corporation and it became known as Vosper Hovermarine Ltd with undercover production at two yards in Woolston. By 1988 the company name had changed to Hovermarine International, but this company went into receivership in January 1997 along with the statement 'In its prime the company employed more than 60 at its factory premises in Southampton, but reductions in light of falling demand resulted in a workforce of only 10 people at the date of receivership. Hovermarine has been involved in the design and manufacture of Hovercraft, rigid side wall craft and fast ferries for more than 30 years and has reportedly sold more than one hundred of these vessels in more than 30 countries around the world'. Eventually International Hovercraft Ltd (IHL) acquired the assets of Hovermarine International Ltd from the receiver. 'In excess of 110 craft -- primarily workhorse HM2 class -- have been built over a period of 25 years. This rugged design, which utilises a hull manufactured in composites with diesel power for both lift and propulsion, proved to be extremely adaptable. Special purpose derivatives of the HM2 design were produced for Tacoma USA and the Port of Rotterdam for firefighting, port surveillance, harbour patrol and hydrographic survey work. Craft have operated in more than forty countries and have proved reliable in service under extreme weather conditions.' In recent times, the site of Hovermarine at Woolston has become home of Griffin Hoverwork.

Vosper VT-1 prototype was large and cumbersome and because it was driven along by water propellers, it could not be beached like a conventional Hovercraft.

The Vosper VT-1 was not a pretty craft. Described as 'semi-amphibious' because it relied for thrust on underwater propellers, it was ponderous and not particularly manoeuvrable. With a two-strong flight crew, it could carry 146 passengers and ten cars at a speed of 40 knots. With a length of 95 feet 6 inches and a beam of 44 feet 6 inches, the power was provided by a pair of 2,000 hp AVCO Lycoming Gas Turbines. Described as a quieter Hovercraft, this was supposed to be because the propulsion propellers were at all times under water, beaching was, of course, impossible, the vessel only being able to nudge its nose ashore.

Bearing the marks G-12-5, the Westland SR.N2 of 1962 was the largest ACV to be built in the world at the time. Initially built without a skirt, it was subsequently provided with a four-foot skirt and in this form carried many thousands of passengers in both Britain and Canada. The most advanced Hovercraft to date, the 4 x 815 hp Nimbus gas-turbine powered SR.N2 prepares to leave its Cowes assembly hangar for the first time to undertake initial engine runs. It would undergo a number of revamps in the course of the following year, the cabin fenestration altering dramatically along with the height and shape of the steerable power pods and the height of the fin.

In 1959, Westland Aircraft bought Saunders-Roe. In 1966 Westland negotiated with rival Hovercraft maker Vickers and agreed that the market was too small for them both so, on March 1st, they merged their Hovercraft interests to form The British Hovercraft Corporation (BHC). In reality Westland held 65% of the shares, Vickers 25% and the remaining 10% were held by the National Research Development Council. Between these two events came the SR.N2 with its dual combined propulsion and lift systems. Each system was powered by a pair of Blackburn Nimbus gas turbines driving a 12-feet 6-inch diameter centrifugal lift fan and a 10-feet diameter Dowty Rotol variable-pitch airscrew. The total provided 3,600 maximum continuous horsepower. Up to 76 passengers or eight tons of freight could be carried.

The first serious attempt by Westland to produce a commercially-operational Hovercraft resulted in the 27-ton 48-passenger SR.N2 of 1961. Powered by four 815 shp Bristol Siddeley Nimbus turbines, this vehicle operated in Britain and Canada as an experimental passenger ferry and managed to carry some 34,000 passengers. Only one was ever built but the experience it provided was second to none.

Encouraged by the sea-trials of the SR.N1, Westland and the Hovercraft Development had agreed to embark on the design and construction of a new project to be on a joint fifty-fifty per cent shared basis. It would be a combined civil and military project as distinct from a mere research vehicle. The outcome was the design and development of the 27-ton passenger-carrying Hovercraft called the SR.N2. By far the largest machine to date, this was a vessel that could travel at a speed of 80 mph over a distance of 200 nautical miles. Powered by four Bristol-Siddeley Nimbus turbine engines, it was 64 feet 8 inches in length and had a width of 29 feet 6 inches. It was still 'pre-skirt' days and the SR.N2 with its curious ship-like bows. Later the hull was modified and a process of skirt-evaluation began. The secret of the practical skirt, however, was not adequately solved until after September 1962.

The Westland-labelled SR.N2 was a practical looking vessel but it was still a primitive attempt and was the wrong undershape to make practical experiments possible with the modification of a skirt. In fact in sea-trials, with its four-foot fully-inflated skirt finally fitted, it proved how easily the one-chamber skirt could be ripped in little more than calm sea.

The SR.N2 fitted with an experimental four-foot all-terrain skirt.

Recording the day! August 13th, 1962 and the first passenger Hovercraft service is about to depart Appley Beach, Ryde, Isle of Wight, for the crossing to Southsea, Portsmouth. The machine is the Westland SR.N2 and the journey time would be just eight minutes.

Looking deceptively small and a little insignificant, Westland's SR.N2 hangs suspended from one of Southampton Harbour's giant ships' cranes on its return from Canada in 1963.

The normally benign Isle of Wight winter weather turned in March 1963 and produced the coldest night in the area for 66 years. Wootton Creek, on the north side of the Island, was choked with pack ice up to 9 inches and ice-floes up to six-feet in length. The SR.N2 was brought out to take advantage of the situation. The 27-ton ACV is seen at sub-zero air and water temperatures. It proved that this sort of weather and sea condition were unlikely to interfere with normal operation of the vessel.

In the early days Hovercraft may have been restricted in altitude and to a certain extent speed but that did not prevent them from globe-trotting. Just as commercial aircraft were tried and tested in foreign climes, so was the Hovercraft. Here in April 1963 we see the SR.N2 being loaded aboard a ship at Southampton for the journey to Montreal for wintertime trials on the St. Laurence River.

At the time of its introduction in 1964, the Westland SR.N3 was the World's largest Hovercraft. Weighing 37.5 tons, it was powered by four 1,050 hp Bristol Siddeley Gnome gas turbine engines. One up from the SR.N2 which was trialled with first a one-foot skirt and later with a four-foot all-terrain skirt.

The SR.N3 was an enlarged development of the SR.N2. It was built for the Interservice Hovercraft Trials Unit (IHTU) and was used for a number of military research and evaluation programmes over land and sea at speeds in excess of 55 mph.

After the virtually circular planform of the SR.N1, and the rectangular SR.N2, the SR.N3 XS655 was an 'evaluation' Hovercraft with directional propellers which were steerable. These paved the way for the highly successful and enormous SR.N4 series. *Picture by courtesy of Stephen Peltz.*

Here we see the SR.N3 Hovercraft undergoing trials at Cowes in 1963 using an experimental interim skirt.

Under the auspices of the Interservice Hovercraft Trials Unit based at Lee-on-Solent, the Westland SR.N3 underwent extensive evaluation tests. This tri-service unit was disbanded in 1971 and was replaced by the Naval Hovercraft Trials Unit (NHTU), itself disbanded in 1981. Between the years 1974-1976, this unit was in the charge of Commander William Russell 'Bill' Hart. *Picture by courtesy of Stephen P Peltz.*

The prototype SR.N4 evolved from the SR.N3. This time no fewer than four steerable airscrews with pivotable twin fins and a simple bag skirt made for a practical vehicle which while yet to be a passenger-friendly vessel, was a major step in that direction. This model would progress through many design stages to become the mainstay of cross-Channel services in the years to come.

A fine study of one of the early British Rail Seaspeed's SR.N4 Hovercraft at sea en route Dover-Calais in 1970.

Press day at Cowes for the launch of the passenger version of the SR.N4 on October 26th 1967. It seemed unthinkable that so vast a vessel could float sideways off the hard-standing and hover over the sea on a cushion of air. The hangar-cum-factory behind is the familiar one-time Saunders-Roe factory where, previously, flying boats such as the Princess were built.

History in the making as the passenger-carrying SR.N4 takes to the sea for the first time at East Cowes on the Isle of Wight. Named *Mountbatten* Class, the SR.N4 was, when it first appeared, the world's largest Hovercraft. Weighing in at 165 tons it had the ability to carry 250 passengers and 30 motor cars on a cross-Channel shuttle service. It would complete the journey from Dover or Ramsgate to France in just 35 minutes. It was launched from the East Cowes works that were originally Saunders-Roe, then Westland Aircraft Ltd and now British Hovercraft Corporation. The date was February 4th, 1968.

Beaching the SR.N4 on its slipway is where the four swivelling propellers come into their own. In this picture it can clearly be seen that the aft airscrews are turned towards the starboard side while the front ones face to port. The effect of this is to turn the vessel through 90 degrees so that it can park (i.e. settle down) facing the viewer close to the waiting ground-crew in the foreground.

Roll-out of the 165-ton SR.N4 at the British Hovercraft Corporation factory at Cowes on October 26th 1967. Built expressly for the cross-Channel service, the world's biggest Hovercraft was powered by four 3,400 shp (shaft horsepower) Bristol Siddeley Marine Proteus gas turbine engines. Typical loads advertised for the craft were 609 passengers (all seated), or 254 passengers and 30 motor-cars, or 50 tons of freight.

An original Hawker Siddeley photograph dated July 17th 1978 and showing the SR.N4 GH-2007, *The Princess Anne*. This was one of two vessels that plied the Channel under the names of Seaspeed and Hoverspeed, and is now preserved at The Hovercraft Museum at Lee-on-Solent.

The Dover cross-Channel terminal with two of the giant SR.N4 Mk.2 Hovercraft in the colours of Hoverspeed on the concrete apron.

Viewed head on, one can get some idea of the sheer bulk of the SR.N4 *The Princess Margaret*. It was certainly an impressive sight as it rode up towards you on its huge skirt.

The SR.N4 Mk.2 was a very large cross-Channel passenger carrier. When the decision to expand it yet further was taken, some felt it a stretch too far and forecast that it would be insufficiently powerful enough. The Mk.3 capacity jumped from 282 passengers and 37 cars to 400 passengers and 60 cars. From a weight of 180 tons with the Mk.1, this had now jumped to 250 tons. Here is *The Princesse Anne* approaching Ramsgate. Later to be known by its registration as GH-2007, this was to become a mainstay of Seaspeed and then Hoverspeed's cross-Channel service.

The cross-Channel service was operated by Hoverlloyd which became Hoverspeed using the huge *Mountbatten* class SR.N4. This machine, GH-2054 *The Prince of Wales*, was the Mk.2 version. Flat out maximum speed was said to be 81 mph but to the present author's knowledge this was only achieved on unmanned test. Capacity was 609 passengers or 254 passengers and 30 cars or 50 tons of freight. Here the vessel is seen operating the Dover-Ramsgate – Calais-Boulogne service.

After the impressive size of the SR.N4 models, the SR.N5 marked a return to more sobre, manageable-sized vessels. Here is the prototype being evaluated between Ryde and Portsmouth. This machine was the first air-cushion vehicle designed to capitalise on skirt technology, but it suffered an unfortunate series of accidents, happily without injury, within a short space of time in 1965. The first happened when being evaluated by Scanhover in Ålesund Harbour in Norway. The pilot was demonstrating an emergency stop when the vessel overturned. Six days later while operating a trial service across the Elbe Estuary in Germany in a strong tail wind, the vessel overshot its base and struck two cars. It was quickly learned that controlling a Hovercraft downwind was one of the most difficult aspects of Hovercraft-piloting to master. Another SR.N5 overturned in San Francisco Bay. While mishap number two may have been pilot error, the other accidents required serious investigation and were finally isolated as due to hydrodynamic suction at the lower edge of the peripheral jet on the side of the bow creating a semi-sideways plough-in. *Picture by courtesy of Stephen P Peltz.*

The SR.N5 underwent an extensive programme of improvements during its lifetime starting with changes to hull nose shape and the deep skirt. Later the twin tail fins were shortened and a third fitted at the front above the cabin. This vessel suffered from extreme skirt attrition which was never fully solved. One possible explanation may have been that the low aspect-ratio skirt, the 36-foot long vessel used a four-feet deep skirt which caused porpoising at a variety of speeds.

The Cowes-built SR.N5 was the first Hovercraft in the world to enter production: it was much smaller than the previous model, the *Mountbatten* class SR.N4. Described as 'a small, high-performance Hovercraft with a wide range of applications, it was a very different machine having a length of only 39 feet. Named *Warden*, it was powered by a single 900 shp Bristol Siddeley Marine Gnome gas turbine which drove both a 7 feet diameter 12-bladed lifting fan and a 9 feet diameter 4-bladed variable-pitch airscrew. Demonstrating the utility and flexibility of this craft, the SR.N5 could travel at 80 mph and tackle a gradient of one in six. Fitted with a four-feet flexible skirt, it could operate over severe mixed terrain including debris-strewn water, ice and the roughest types of ground. If the *Mountbatten* Class employed something like 80 hp to every ton of the machine's total weight, the *Warden* Class SR.N5 developed 130 hp per ton.

Westland SR.N5-006 of British Hovercraft Corporation sits on its skirt on a gravel beach.

Westland's SR.N5 underwent extensive military trials in 1963-4 and here is a picture of one, marked XT492, on manoeuvres. Note the top gunner, the wireless aerials and the radar installation. These trials involved two machines, the other being XT493 which was rebuilt as a SR.N6 *Winchester*. *Picture by courtesy of Stephen P Peltz.*

Westland SR.N5 with a full load of passengers travelling at speed on a moderate sea. The short body length made for a fairly bumpy ride in rough water conditions. This model would go on to be built in America under licence by the Bell Helicopter Company as the Westland-Bell SK-5 Jet Skimmer.

American makers quickly cottoned on to the Hovercraft, one of these being Bell which built one of the first all-American models in the form of this SK-5 Jet Skimmer. The first air-cushion vehicle to enter service in America, this was a licence-built version of the Cowes-built Westland SR.N5. Slightly different in detail but unmistakably from Cowes, this was operated by San Francisco & Oakland Helicopter Airlines, better known as SFO Helicopter. This was a carrier founded in 1961 to offer scheduled passenger flights around San Francisco, Oakland and other Bay-area townships. One of the earliest US helicopter services to operate without a federal subsidy, it was also the first to use turbine-only helicopters. It began Hovercraft services at the beginning of August 1965 carrying passengers between the International Airports of Oakland and San Francisco or downtown San Francisco with a 15-seat Westland-Bell SK-5 and appeared to enjoy good business and rapid growth. Promoted as carrying its passengers on a four-foot deep air cushion, each 20-mile leg of the route took about 16 minutes. In 1969, it was reputed to have carried 320,000 passengers on more than 100 flights a day but the airline was declared bankrupt in July 1970 and had disappeared by 1986.

The Americans were surprisingly upbeat about the potential of the Hovercraft as this press photo of SFO passengers disembarking at Oakland International Airport relates. 'The Jet Skimmer is being tested by the Federal Government in conjunction with SFO Helicopter Airlines, who [sic] operates the craft, the Port of Oakland and Bell Aerosystems Company to determine its capabilities in serving commuter runs throughout the country'.

The Americans picked up quite quickly on Hovercraft technology and in the early 1970s they began a programme called Landing Craft Air Cushion (LCAC), a generic term for a military assault Hovercraft. One of the ones they built was the AVCO Lycoming TF40, pictured here. Some 88 feet in length and weighing 87 tons, the five-crew vessel entered service in 1986. A novel feature was that the Hovercraft could be stowed on a well-deck in an amphibious parent ship so that it could be deployed on and off an assault vessel. The picture shows 'LCAC-1' and a very large front cushion-skirt – but where, one wonders, is the bridge?

Flight's supplement for July 25th, 1963, is tellingly introduced by what is clearly a capital indictment for the US Hovercraft industry. Over a picture of the Bell Systems SKMR-1 Hydroskimmer Hovercraft trials on Lake Erie (seen here), the editor states: 'Whereas UK companies put ACV research high on their agendas, this cannot be said of the Americans who, despite their huge research and investment into aeronautics, largely left the ACV either to back-yard experimenters or to manufacturers who appear to have constructed hardware first and thought about it afterwards. Under the unattractive appellation of ground-effect machine or GEM, American workers having tending to create ACVs whose performances [sic] is less convincing that the publicity with which they have been promoted,' So reads the introduction to this image of the Bell SKMR-1 Hydroskimmer, a surprisingly late starter in the military experimental vehicle field designed and built at Bell Aerospace Corporation's Wheatfield plant in Buffalo, NY, for the US Navy Bureau of Ships. This, the second experimental vehicle made by Bell, was 18 feet in length and cruised at 40 knots above Lake Eerie – at that time the maximum speed allowed on the lake.

After the enormity of the SR.N4 Westland reverted to Hovercraft of a less-challenging size with the SR.N6. This came in a number of styles and forms. Here is a basic passenger-carrying model being built at the Cowes factory.

Westland SR.N6-009 operated by British Hovercraft Corporation giving a display at a South Coast air display. The '009' part of the designation is the serial number showing that it is the ninth example to have been built. Also worth pointing out is that after the formal foundation of the designation 'Saunders-Roe Nautical No. 1', the Cowes firm was not always consistent in referring to its products as 'SR.N6', SRN-6' or 'SRN.6', the inference being that all are correct!

Extensive sea trials off Southampton preceded the opening of a Southampton-Cowes public service.

SR.N6 on trials manoeuvres in restricted space on the River Itchen.

Trials far from home. SR.N6 on loan to the British Malayan Petroleum Company Ltd, Borneo.

The SR.N6 was the most successful of all Hovercraft to be manufactured anywhere in the World. They have been the mainstay of the small time ferry operators as well as the bastion of Hovercraft service. Known as the *Winchester* class, the design was systematically improved and enlarged over the years of their service.

Trials with servicing a North-Sea oil rig. This proved more difficult than expected for continuous rough water and pitching seas posed a real and continuous danger to the Hovercraft which experienced difficulty getting close enough without damaging the skirt. Here we see an SR.N6 trying it out. Oil-rig servicing (meaning supply and staffing) became virtually exclusively the prerogative of the helicopter due to problems such as this.

More military trials, this time with XT657, a shortened variant of the SR.N6 *Winchester*. The starboard side of the nose reveals a patch over a long rip following some ham-fisted handling. *Picture by courtesy of Stephen P Peltz.*

On the hard at Portsmouth-Southsea Hovercraft terminal, one of the SR.N6 vessels lifts on its skirt with the front door open.

SR.N6 *Sea Hawk* operated by Seaspeed working the Cowes-Southampton passenger service. Note the British Rail logo on the forward cabin roof. Seaspeed was set up in November 1965 by British Rail Hovercraft Ltd, as a rather unwilling operator of Hovercraft. Contemporary with this was the nascent Hoverlloyd at Ramsgate. *Sea Hawk* was the ninth SR.N6 to be built. After the passing of The Hovercraft Act 1968, all Hovercraft had to be registered and carry registration markings in the form of the letters GH followed by a hyphen and then a four-digit numeral starting with 'GH-2001' - actually a registration not issued. *Sea Hawk*, seen here, was GH-2014. Note the additional length at the rear of the passenger cabin.

The SR.N6 gave good service between Ryde and Portsmouth. Here one of Hovertravel's vessels is seen on the sands at Ryde taking on and disembarking passengers. In the background, left, can be seen Ryde Pier.

A once-renowned Isle of Wight firm was picture-post-card maker J Arthur Dixon. Born near Keighley in Yorkshire in 1897, John Arthur Dixon went to the Island in 1926 and strove to make a living as a jobbing printer and greeting-card-maker. In 1951 he moved to spacious premises off the Forest Road in Newport, and died in 1958. The company flourished and one of its contemporary post-cards is this showing the SR.N6 coming ashore on the sands on the east side of Ryde Pier. Dixons faded into obscurity in recent times following various hostile take-over bids, vanishing in 2000.

Keeping the cross-Channel SR.N6 fresh between trips was sometimes a disagreeable chore especially after a rough crossing had caused a degree of sickness on board. Here we see some between-trips maintenance.

An evocative snapshot from the *Carisbrooke Castle* showing the Seaspeed SR.N6 Hovercraft en passage. In the background is the $\frac{1}{4}$-mile long Royal Victoria Hospital at Netley near Southampton. Opened in 1856 and built with a quarter of a million bricks, it was the largest brick structure in Britain. The significance is that it was pulled down in September 1966, merely the Chapel left to mark its existence. The picture was taken on September 25th, 1966.

Saunders-Roe SR.N6 at Ryde in September 1969. The vessel is supported on trestles to allow repairs to the skirt which is detached at the bows.

The military version of the popular passenger vessel was a different shape. British Army's Westland SR.N6 *Winchester* Class Hovercraft XV614 of No.200 Sqdn RCT/IHTU was one of a batch of four supplied for joint service trials. There were marked changes between this version and the popular civilian passenger variant.

British Rail's Southampton-Cowes (Isle of Wight) service was operated using the SR.N6 Hovercraft. Here can be seen one of these craft entering the River Itchen at Southampton on Tuesday, July 5th 1966 – a rehearsal for the start of the service later that day. The VIP passengers on board included Alderman Mitchell, Mayor of Southampton, and the chairman of the British Railways Board, Stanley Raymond. The service was to be hourly in each direction.

The SR.N6 *Winchester* was also used by the Royal Navy. Reinforced decking to enable 20 fully-armed and equipped servicemen to be carried on either side and some judiciously-positioned armour-plating made the machine into an ideal combat vessel. A roof hatch in the control cabin allowed a machine gun and its operator to be carried 'topside' and the maximum capacity was 38. The cushion depth was such that it would safely negotiate walls and obstructions six feet in height. Due to the added weight, the military SR.N6 was not as fast as civilian models but its lift was increased. XV859 was the sole example and it is seen here pictured in 1978.

Very much at the other end of the scale, the Borneo-based British Malayan Petroleum Company Limited used its SR.N6 for exploration duties and transit across swamps. In this picture the engine is running and the skirt partially inflated on residual pressure. Note the easy-access nose door and ramp.

The SR.N6 was to enjoy considerable popularity overseas and were employed in almost every corner of the world. First exhibited at Canada's Expo '67, it attracted great interest from the frozen wastes dividing Sweden from Denmark (where one later operated a regular summertime passenger service between Hälsingborg and Helsingør across the northern end of the Øresund) to the icy waters off Iceland (where Icelandic authorities explored its capabilities in the field of coastal fishery protection). This example, SR.N6-014, was used by the British Malayan Petroleum Company Limited in Borneo. It is pictured here with company executives. Observe the dark shorts as worn by senior management!

The British Hovercraft Corporation was the name of the umbrella-organisation created to embrace all official UK Hovercraft activities when Saunders-Roe, the division of Westland Aircraft and Vickers Supermarine combined forces in March 1966 with the aim of establishing one viable commercial Hovercraft industry. As regards 'work in hand', none of the Vickers projects were moved forward and the new company concentrated on the SR.N5 *Warden* Class, the SR.N6 *Winchester* Class and the SR.N4 *Mountbatten* Class Hovercraft. Only one new design was produced in 1969 by the British Hovercraft Corporation and this was the BH.7 *Wellington* Class. In 1970 Westland Aircraft acquired the shares of the other parties and the following year acquired Cushioncraft company from Britten-Norman. By 1984 the company name was changed to Westland Aerospace - Hovercraft design/manufacture had effectively ceased and the company was involved with the manufacture of composites for the Aerospace industry. The British Hovercraft Corporation was responsible for the largest Union Flag in the world. It was painted on the doors of their hangar on the seafront at East Cowes in 1977 to celebrate the Silver Jubilee of the Queen.

KW255 was a British Hovercraft Corporation's BH-7 *Warden* Class Hovercraft for military evaluation in 1960.

The British Hovercraft Corporation's AP1-88 is a medium size Hovercraft that can seat up to 101 passengers. With a crew of three, the Westland-designed vessel has been used on routes in Britain as well as from Sweden to Denmark. In trooping format it can carry up to 90 troops while in military logistics mode it can carry two Land Rovers, a Bv202 tracked vehicle, and trailer unit or about 10 tons (10,000 kg) of stores. It has also been supplied to Canada where it has been used by the Canadian Coast Guard. Here we see an early example in the colours of Hovertravel completing a Southsea-Ryde crossing.

The Westland-built Type 299AP1-88 was 24.5 metres long, 11.2 metres wide and had a full-load displacement of 47.6 tons. Power was provided by four 600 hp Deutz AG diesel engines which provided both lift and propulsion. Propulsion used a pair of three-bladed variable-pitch ducted airscrews.

A British Hovercraft Corporation BH-7 Mk.2 is seen here in September 1963 engaged in a month-long series of trials at HMS *Osprey*, later renamed *Daedalus*, at Portland on the South Coast. The purpose was to explore the Hovercraft's unique mine countermeasures advantages which included invulnerability, high speed, high controllability and low cost. Mine warfare countermeasures at that time represented a high-budget operation. Because of the Hovercraft's low 'underwater signatures', magnetic, acoustic and pressure, the Hovercraft had proved virtually immune to underwater explosions and, for a mine-hunting Hovercraft, it was up to 50% cheaper than conventional vessels. The machine seen here was equipped with a Plessey Marine 193 Sonar and a 2048 Speedscan installation as well as being fitted out with Racal-Decca Trisponder navigation equipment.

With a smartly-turned-out crew standing rigidly to attention, the 1969 British Hovercraft Corporation BH-7 Hovercraft, serial number XW255, entered service with the Royal Navy for a number of trials, none of which convinced the powers-that-be that it was viable for the tasks assigned to it. It was later acquired by the Hovercraft Museum at Lee-on-Solent.

Hovercraft Development Ltd's HD1 fitted with hybrid skirt and travelling at speed.

British Hovercraft's AP188 ferry comes to the rescue of Scandinavian Airlines! Early in 1985 the vessel began carrying 100 passengers per trip on the Copenhagen (Denmark) to Malmo (Sweden) route having seen business decline In 1972 200,000 passengers had been transported but by 1983 this had fallen to just 40,000. In 1984 SAS began a Hovercraft service across the Øresund Sound, the 17-mile trip taking just 45 minutes. Key to the operation was a new low-pressure skirt system which increased payload by up to 50%. The AP188 was powered by four 450 hp Deutz diesel engines combining both lift and propulsion. Two diesels provided power to four centrifugal lift fans and to drive the craft's flexed propulsion propellers. A pair of rotating bow thrusters helped steer the vessel into its quick-entry docking facilities. In 1984, the company had taken more than 100,000 passengers, a result which inspired the company to explore designs for 140-200 seaters.

Built for military trials, the BH.7 XH255 was known as the *Wellington* Class by builders British Hovercraft Corporation, successors to Saunders-Roe Ltd and Westland Aircraft Ltd. The next design up from the SR.N6, the BH.7 weighed 18.3 tons, displaced 56 tons and was 78 feet in length with a beam of 45 feet. Power was provided by one 4,250 shp (shaft horsepower) Rolls-Royce Marine Proteus gas turbine which provided both lift and propulsion and drove one four-bladed variable-pitch airscrew. The speed was 58 knots. Capacity was 60 troops and a crew of three. First flown in November 1969 it was evaluated by the Royal Navy – one of the last Hovercraft to operate with a military aircraft serial number.

The passenger-carrying SR.N4 became the mainstay of the cross-Channel Hovercraft ferry service. This was always good for a picture-story and many press photographs were taken to keep the service in the public eye. Here's one from the summer of 1972 showing SR.N4 *The Princess Anne* at Boulogne. The highly-technical caption tells us that 'Rolls Royce engines activate propellers which scoot craft of [sic] asphalt and across water on a cushion of air'.

After the Saunders-Roe factory was taken over by Westlands it bore that name for a while until, with the coming of the British Hovercraft Corporation, it was repainted, unfortunately all in lower-case letters in the fashion of the age. Here we see a SR.N4 occupying a major part of the slip-way.

The International Hoverport at Ramsgate, better known to all and sundry as Pegwell Bay in Kent. Centrestage is Hoverlloyd's SR.N45 GH-2005 named *Sure*.

Ramsgate in Kent became the jumping-off point for the Hovercraft service across the Channel and this air-to-ground view gives a good general idea of the size of the base and also the sheer size of the SR.N4 Mk. 2.

Another photograph of those great doors at the Columbine Works, Cowes. This one is very interesting, though, for other reasons. First, besides being painted up for Westland Aircraft Ltd, it shows the special Hovercraft slipway or ramp which was specially made and widened for launching the SR.N4. It also shows on the ramp the SR.N3, XS655, built for Naval evaluation. Moored by the lower jetty is the Denny sidewall Hovercraft undergoing comparative tests at Cowes. Sharp-eyed observers will also spy the helicopter landing area marked out on the apron.

The Denny sidewall Hovercraft, seen here on trails at Gareloch, Firth of Clyde, in May 1961, seemed to encapsulate all the limitations associated with a sidewall craft only starting with the impossibility of beaching.

Unlike the air-cushion vehicles, a variation was the sidewall craft. Here the Hovercraft hull bore some resemblance to the catamaran in that the hull comprised two rigid side walls which protruded downwards into the water. The air curtain was only essential at the rear of the hull. As the craft accelerated through the water, air was naturally compressed through the channel at the bow comprising the two sidewalls and the bottom of the hull and the surface of the water. The air curtain at the rear served to aid in lifting the craft while containing the 'ram-air' effect brought about by speed. Of course this was not an amphibious craft and was restricted to sea-going. The first successful sidewall craft was the D.1 built by the William Denny & Brothers Co of Clydeside. That was in 1960. Pictured here is the 18-ton HM.2, a product of Hovermarine Ltd at Southampton, which was intended to carry 60 to 65 passengers at speeds up to 40 mph. It entered scheduled service with British Rail Hovercraft Ltd and operated their Seaspeed service between Portsmouth and Ryde, Isle of Wight. Here it is seen undergoing trials off Southampton in February 1968. BRH Ltd was a joint company between British Rail and the French SNCF set up in 1965. In reality, the Portsmouth-Ryde service was more suited to the SR.N4 and N6 vessels.

Operating a trial service on the River Thames is the Denny Hoverbus in 1963. The legend written on the side reads 'Thames Launches Ltd – A Denny Hovercraft'.

Built in Scotland by shipbuilders Denny of Dumbarton, the D1 was an early 1960s-vintage sidewall craft which was transported by road to Southampton for evaluation. Due to the inherent limitations imposed by the sidewall philosophy it was not proceeded with. This picture was taken in March 1962.

The Hovercraft bug quickly spread around the world and caught many along the way. Here is a Japanese student who made this single-seat hover car, one of the many early skirtless craft to have appeared in the corners of the globe.

Nearer to home, France as ever had its rich sub-culture of talented inventors. Jacques and Jean Grimaldi built this flying saucer Hovercraft in February 1962. Nothing further is known about it.

A talented amateur, Don Robertson of Kingswood, Sussex, built three small Hovercraft between 1960 and 1965, and tested them at Redhill Aerodrome. He was chairman of a company called Hovertravel.

Don Robertson demonstrates his Skimmer on the grass in front of the hangars at Redhill.

An attempt at a family sporting Hovercraft was displayed at the Earls Court Boat Show at the end of 1963. This was the so-called 'Hoverbout' a small-sized vessel built at the Cornubia Yacht Yard, Clarence Road, East Cowes by C E Clark (Cowes) Ltd. This was a now-defunct specialist boat yard which built yachts to the design of top men such as Robert Tucker and Uffa Fox. Powered by a converted Hillman Imp engine, Hoverbout was 16 feet long, 10 feet wide and was estimated to sell for £1,500 when in full production. A contemporary description describes the engine as being: 'a conversion of a well-known car engine, only complicated by such additional devices as pumps, special cooling and exhaust systems.'

C E Clark's Hoverbout Hovercraft on trials on the River Medina at Cowes in 1963. Both the project and its makers disappeared soon after.

The Americans were very quick indeed at attempting to make a consumer product out of the Hovercraft and in November 1960 a Mr. Charles Rhodes of Pittsburgh, Pennsylvania, arrived here with his 250cc two-cylinder Yamaha-powered Hover-Scooter. Seen here being demonstrated at Thames Ditton in Surrey under the auspices of the British magazine *The Motor Cycle*, the skirtless vehicle appears to fly very close to the terrain.

In January 1962 it was revealed than the Swedish company Saab was developing, in great secrecy a Hovercraft. When it appeared in 1963 it emerged as a practical little cabin two-seater with a length of 7.3m, a width of 3.1m and powered by a 180hp aircooled four-cylinder Lycoming O-360-A1A aircraft engine turning an eight-bladed fan 1.6m in diameter. With an empty weight of 1,500 kg, the Saab 401 had a cruising speed of 75 km/hr at a maximum hover height of 17 cm. The hull was of composite construction. No skirt was ever fitted. Early on the machine was remodelled as an occasional four-seater and secondary propulsion engines provided. These were in the form of a pair of McCulloch four-cylinder two-strokes each of 72 hp. A rare survivor, the Saab 401 is currently stored at the Karlskrona Marinmuseum.

The Royal Air Force Cadets at Cranwell made themselves a Hovercraft in 1963. Their CH-1 has no skirt and was mainly circular which made it ideal for random pondering around RAF flower beds.

To mark the fifteenth anniversary of Cockerell's invention, London's Central Office of Information produced this picture of the giant *Mountbatten* Class SR.N4.with the story that 'from small beginnings a new industry has been developed. Regular Hovercraft services have now been running in Britain for three years and many new routes are being opened at home and abroad. The vast £1,750,000 SR.N4 – the world's biggest Hovercraft and the world's first Hovercraft car-ferry - made its maiden English Channel crossing recently, taking only 36 minutes to reach Boulogne. Hovermarine Ltd have launched their 60-seater HM2 sidewall craft and plans for tracked Hovercraft (hovertrain) have been announced'. The picture is dated Dover, June 1968.

The cavernous maw of Hoverlloyd's SR.N6 *Swift* on the foreshore at Pegwell Bay. Notice, for comparison, the relative size of the BP Bowser at the right.

An unusual but very important use of the Hovercraft principle is its use in aircraft recovery. Where an aircraft has suffered undercarriage collapse or perhaps has veered off the runway onto soft ground, speedy recovery is vital to ensure the minimum inconvenience to airport operation while at the same time imparting as little additional damage to the incapacitated aircraft. Where 'time is money', a busy airport cannot afford to have a runway blocked for a minute longer than necessary, so having equipment to move potential blockages is not just important – it's crucial. Two Southampton-based companies joined forces to produce suitable equipment – Air Cushion Equipment Ltd and Aero Docks Ltd. Here a surplus DC4 Argonaut, G-ALHJ, is seen supported on inflatable air bags on a system of hover platforms. The load can now be moved easily in any direction irrespective of the terrain. This picture was taken on March 24th, 1970.